# SPANISH MADE EASY

By
*Diego A. Agúndez*
*Rashmi Varma*

# GOODWILL PUBLISHING HOUSE®
**B-3 Rattan Jyoti, 18 Rajendra Place,**
**NEW DELHI- 110 008 (INDIA)**

*Published by*
**GOODWILL PUBLISHING HOUSE®**
*B-3 Rattan Jyoti, 18 Rajendra Place*
*New Delhi-110008 (INDIA)*
*Tel. : 25750801, 25820556*
*Fax : 91-11-25764396*
*E-mail : goodwillpub@vsnl.net*
        *ylp@bol.net.in*
*Website : www.goodwillpublishinghouse.com*

*Printed at :*
B.B. Press
Noida

# A Nuestros Padres

# To Our Parents

# COUNTRIES WHICH HAVE SPANISH AS THEIR OFFICIAL LANGUAGE

Argentina

Chile

Paraguay

Uruguay

Bolivia

Ecuador

Peru

Venezuela

Colombia

Panama

Guatemala

Costa Rica

Honduras

Nicaragua

El Salvador

Dominican Republic

Cuba

Mexico

Spain

Equatorial Guinea

West Sahara Territory

# PREFACE

Spanish is the most widely spoken language among the romantic branches of the Indo-European languages. Language of love, literature and passion, it is spoken by more than 300 million people in the world, mainly in America and Southern Europe, with Spain, Mexico, Argentina, Colombia and even the United States as the main centres of usage.

Although its presence in Asia is limited to a few communities in Philippines, the importance of Spanish in the world is increasing due to the growing economical power of Spain (8$^{th}$ highest world economy). In the United States, Spanish is the second official language, with more than 40 million speakers.

This book has been written by Rashmi Varma and Diego A. Agúndez, who have considerable experience in teaching foreign languages and have also authored *French made easy* and *German made easy* in this collection.

The book is ideal for those who are learning this language without a teacher. The idea of this book was never to be an in-depth study of the language; but rather, a brief on the pronunciation and grammar, and a collection of set phrases which would help the readers while travelling around the world.

Language learning should be quick, fun and easy! This book provides you with the vocabulary with which you can create new sentences, sentence patterns, correct pronunciation and dialogues, which will help you communicate in different situations. Whatever has motivated you to learn the language, *SPANISH MADE EASY* will help you to achieve these goals.

So, let's start speaking Spanish.

# CONTENTS

# 1
# INTRODUCTION
## *INTRODUCCIÓN*

There are 29 letters in Spanish and all are pronounced differently from the English alphabet. It is interesting to know that the letters K and W are used only in words taken from other languages. Pay special attention to the letter Ñ that does not exist in rest of the languages.

| | |
|---|---|
| A | *aa* |
| B | *bay* |
| C | *say* |
| CH | *chay* |
| D | *day* |
| E | *ay* |
| F | *efe* |
| G | *khay* |
| H | *achay* |
| I | *ee* |
| J | *khota* |
| K | *kah* |
| L | *ele* |
| LL | *a-ye* |

| | | |
|---|---|---|
| M | | *eme* |
| N | | *ene* |
| Ñ | | *enyay* |
| O | | *o* |
| P | | *pay* |
| Q | | *koo* |
| R | | *erre* |
| S | | *ese* |
| T | | *tay* |
| U | | *oo* |
| V | | *oobe* |
| W | | *oobe-doble* |
| X | | *ekees* |
| Y | | *a-ye* |
| Z | | *seta* |

\* 'H' in Spanish has no sound. We do write it, but it is silent.

'Y' used on its own, means 'and'.

'O' used on its own, means 'or'.

## PRONUNCIATION                      CONSONANTS

| | | |
|---|---|---|
| [b] | B | *bomba* |
| | V | *vaca* |
| [d] | D | *donde, caldo* |
| [ð] | d | *cada, pardo* |
| [f] | F | *faro, gafas* |
| [g] | G | *grande, guinda* |
| [k] | C | *cosa* |
| | QU | *queso* |

|        | K   | *kiosco*           |
|--------|-----|--------------------|
| [l]    | L   | *ala, luz*         |
| [m]    | M   | *madre, cama*      |
| [n]    | N   | *no, pena*         |
| [p]    | P   | *país, campo*      |
| [r]    | R   | *altar, paro*      |
| *[rr]* | R   | *rosa, rico*       |
|        | RR  | *perro, carro*     |
| [s]    | S   | *solo, paso*       |
| [è]    | C   | *cera*             |
|        | Z   | *cazo*             |
| [t]    | T   | *tarta, toro*      |
| [tò]   | CH  | *chocolate, ocho*  |
| [h]    | Ñ   | *niña*             |
| [x]    | g   | *gema*             |
|        | j   | *jamón*            |
| *[ë]*  | ll  | *llave, collar*    |

## VOWELS

|     |   |                 |
|-----|---|-----------------|
| [i] | i | *imagen, piso*  |
| [e] | e | *eso, tela*     |
| [a] | a | *amigo, pata*   |
| [o] | o | *bolo, otro*    |
| [u] | u | *una, luz*      |

## SEMI VOWELS

|     |    |         |
|-----|----|---------|
| [w] | ua | *agua*  |
|     | hu | *hueso* |

| [j] | i | *miedo* |
| | hi | *hierba* |

## DIPTONGOS

| [ei] | ey | *ley* |
| | ei | *peine* |
| [ai] | ai | *aire, caiga* |
| [oi] | oy | *soy* |
| | oi | *boina* |
| [au] | au | *causa, aula* |
| [eu] | eu | *Europa, feudo* |

*Note* : It is important to keep in mind that @ (which is repeatedly used in this book to facilitate the comprehension of the reader is not a part of the Spanish language) is to be replaced by O in the case of masculine and A in the case of feminine.

*Example* : If you come across the word perr@, it means
Perro (a male dog)
Perra (a female dog)

In Spanish to show a question, a question mark (?) is added at the end of the phrase and an inverted question mark (¿) is added at the beginning of the phrase.

*eg.* ¿Como estás?
How are you?

Similarly, to show an exclamatory phrase, an exclamation mark is added at the end and an inverted exclamation mark is added at the beginning of the phrase.

*eg.* ¡Hola!
Hi!

# 2
# PRESENTATION
## *PRESENTACIÓN*

## PRESENT YOURSELF

My name is Telmo.
*Me llamo Telmo.*

I am 40 years old.
*Tengo cuarenta años.*

I live in India, in New Delhi.
*Vivo en la India, en Nueva Delhi.*

I am an Indian.
*Soy indi@.*

I am a student.
*Soy estudiante.*

I work with IBM.
*Trabajo en IBM.*

I speak Hindi, English and German.
*Hablo hindi, inglés y alemán.*

I am vegetarian.
*Soy vegetarian@.*

## PRESENT A THIRD PERSON (MASCULINE)

His name is Jorge.
*Se llama Jorge.*

He is 24 years old.
*Tiene veinticuatro años.*

He lives in Spain, in Seville.
*Vive en España, en Sevilla.*

He is Spanish.
*Es español.*

He is a businessman.
*Es empresario / Es un hombre de negocios.*

He works with Indicaa Global.
*Trabaja en Indicaa Global.*

He speaks Spanish and French.
*Habla español y francés.*

## PRESENT A THIRD PERSON (FEMININE)

Her name is Ciri.
*Se llama Ciri.*

She is 20 years old.
*Tiene veinte años.*

She is American.
*Es estadounidense.*

She is a housewife.
*Es ama de casa.*

She lives in U.S.A., in New York.
*Vive en Estados Unidos, en Nueva York.*

She speaks Italian and Chinese.
*Habla italiano y chino.*

# 3
# GREETINGS AND EXPRESSIONS
## SALUDOS y EXPRESIONES

Good morning.
*Buenos días.*

Good afternoon.
*Buenas tardes.*

Good evening.
*Buenas tardes.*

Good night.
*Buenas noches.*

Hi / Hello.
*Hola.*

Yes.
*Sí.*

No.
*No.*

Please.
*Por favor.*

Thank you.
*Gracias.*

Sorry.
*Lo siento.*

Welcome!
*¡Bienvenido!*

(7)

Many thanks!
*¡Muy agradecido!*

Pardon.
*Perdón.*

Goodbye.
*Adiós.*

See you tomorrow.
*Hasta mañana.*

Never mind.
*No importa.*

Congratulations.
*Felicidades.*

Happy journey.
*Buen viaje.*

Have a good meal.
*Buen provecho.*

Please repeat.
*¿Puede repetir, por favor?*

See you soon.
*Hasta pronto.*

That's enough.
*Basta ya.*

I have had enough of you.
*Ya te he soportado bastante.*

Have a seat. (Formal)
*Siéntese*

Have a seat. (Informal)
*Siéntate.*

Please come in.
*Entre, por favor.*

Be careful.
*Ten cuidado.*

Wait a minute!
*¡Un momento!*

How are you? (Formal)
*¿Cómo está usted?*

How are you? (Informal)
*¿Qué tal estás?*

I am fine, thank you.
*Estoy bien, gracias.*

How are things going?
*¿Cómo va eso?*

Everything is fine.
*Todo va bien.*

What is your name? (Formal)
*¿Cómo se llama usted?*

What is your name? (Informal)
*¿Cómo te llamas?*

My name is Robert.
*Me llamo Robert.*

How old are you? (Formal)
*¿Qué edad tiene usted?*

How old are you? (Informal)
*¿Cuántos años tienes?*

I am 10 years old.
*Tengo diez años.*

Where do you live? (Formal)
*¿Dónde vive usted?*

Where do you live? (Informal)
*¿Dónde vives?*

I live in Piccadilly Circus.
*Vivo en la Plaza Piccadilly.*

What is your nationality? (Formal)
*¿Cuál es su nacionalidad?*

What is your nationality? (Informal)
*¿Cuál es tu nacionalidad?*

I am an Indian.
*Soy indi@.*

Which country do you come from?
*¿De qué país eres?*

I come from India.
*Soy de la India.*

Are you married?
*¿Está usted casad@?*

Yes, I am married.
*Sí, estoy casad@.*

No, I am a bachelor / spinster.
*No, estoy solter@.*

I have two children.
*Tengo dos hij@s.*

What does this mean?
*¿Qué quiere decir eso?*

Do you speak Spanish?
*¿Habla usted español?*

I speak a little Spanish.
*Hablo un poco de español.*

Do you speak English?
*¿Habla usted inglés?*

Are you busy?
*¿Está usted ocupado?*

No, I am free.
*No, estoy libre.*

I am busy.
*Estoy ocupado.*

Do you smoke?
*¿Fuma usted?*

What are you doing?
*¿Qué hace usted?*

What does your father do?
*¿Qué hace tu padre?*

What does your mother do?
*¿Qué hace tu madre?*

Glad to know you.
*Encantado de conocerl@.*

I/we'd like to.
*Me/Nos gustaría.*

Can I / Can we?
*¿Puedo? / ¿Podemos?*

There is / There are
*Hay*

There isn't / aren't
*No hay*

Now
*Ahora*

Later
*Más tarde*

Before
*Antes*

After
*Después*

Always
*Siempre*

Never
*Nunca*

Sometimes
*A veces*

Often
*A menudo*

Then
*Entonces*

Enough
*Suficiente*

Lots of
*Much@*

All
*Tod@*

Everybody
*Tod@s*

Nobody
*Nadie*

Everywhere
*Por todas partes*

Nowhere
*En ninguna parte*

Everything
*Todo*

Nothing
*Nada*

Something
*Algo*

# 4
## ACCENTS
### *ACENTOS*

An accent is a small diagonal line from upper right to lower left.

Accents serve two purposes in Spanish. Firstly, they indicate where the stress or emphasis falls on a word when it is pronounced and secondly, they help to differentiate between identically spelled words.

The following rules facilitate the pronunciation of words as they tell you on which syllable of the word the stress occurs.

An accent mark is normally not required if:

(i)  The word ends with a vowel (**a, e, i, o, u,**) or **-n** or **-s** and the stress falls on the penultimate syllable. *Examples*:

*Plato* → PLA-to (plate) ends with a vowel and the stress falls on the penultimate syllable.

*Comen* → CO-men (they eat) ends with **-n** and the stress falls on the penultimate syllable.

*Chicas* → CHI-cas (girls) ends with **-s** and the stress falls on the penultimate syllable.

(ii) The word ends with a consonant other than **-n** or **-s** and the stress falls on the last syllable.

*Example*:

> *Hablar* → ha-BLAR (to speak) ends with a **-r** and the stress falls on the last syllable.

> *Canal* → ca-NAL (channel) ends with a **-l** and the stress falls on the last syllable.

An accent is necessary in a situation other than the above two cases. Thus, an accent is required in the following cases:

(i) The word ends with a vowel (**a, e, i, o, u**) or **-n** or **-s** and the stress falls on the last syllable.
*Examples*:

> *Mamá* → ma-MÁ (mama) ends with a vowel and the stress falls on the last syllable.

> *Habitación* → habita-CIÓN (room) ends with a **-n** and the stress falls on the last syllable.

> *Comerás* → come-RÁS (you will eat) ends with a -s and the stress falls on the last syllable.

(ii) The word ends with a consonant other than **-n** or **-s** and the stress falls on the penultimate syllable.
*Examples*:

> *Suéter* → SUÉ-ter (sweater) ends with a **-r** and the stress falls on the penultimate vowel.

(iii) The stress falls on any vowel more than two syllables away from the end of the word.
*Examples*:

> *Miércoles* → MIÉR-co-les (Wednesday) the stress is on the third syllable from the end of the word.

(iv) The stress falls on a weak vowel (**i** or **u**) which is preceded or followed by a strong vowel (**a**, **e**, **o**). *Examples*:

Tío → TÍ-o (uncle) the stress falls on -**i** which is a weak vowel and is followed by -**o** which is a strong vowel.

Accents help to differentiate some words from the ones that are identically spelled. There are three such groups of words and in all the cases, the more emphatic word of the pair carries the accent.

(v) The question and exclamation words carry an accent whereas their corresponding relative pronouns or connecting words do not:

| | | | | |
|---|---|---|---|---|
| *¿dónde?* | where? | ← → | *donde* | where |
| *¿adónde?* | to where? | | *adonde* | to where |
| *¿cómo?* | how? | | *como* | as, like, because |
| *¿cuál?* | which? | | *cual* | which, as |
| *¿cuándo?* | when? | | *cuando* | when |
| *¿cuánto?* | how much? how many? | | *cuanto* | as much, as many |
| *¿qué?* | what? how? | | *que* | which, that |
| *¿quiénes?* | who? whom? | | *quienes* | who, whom |

*Examples*:

| | |
|---|---|
| *¿**Cómo** estás?* | → How are you? |
| *¿**Dónde** está mi mujer?* | → Where is my wife? |
| *¿**Cuál** es tu número de teléfono?* | → What is your telephone number? |
| *Cuando trabajo estoy cansado.* | → When I work, I get tired. |
| *Sé **que** es muy difícil.* | → I know that it is very difficult. |

*Dime **cuanto** sepas.* → Tell me as much as you know.

(vi) The accents are used to differentiate between the demonstrative pronouns and the demonstrative adjectives. Earlier the demonstrative adjectives did not carry an accent whereas the demonstrative pronouns did. Now, both of them are accepted without accent, but it's still correct to put the accent over the pronouns.

| | | | | |
|---|---|---|---|---|
| éste | ésta | éstos | éstas | this one, these |
| ése | ésa | ésos | ésas | that one, those |
| aquél | aquélla | aquéllos | aquéllas | that one, those |
| este | esta | estos | estas | this, these |
| ese | esa | esos | esas | that, those |
| aquel | aquella | aquellos | aquellas | that, those |

esto

eso (this/that thing, matter, business)

aquello

*Examples*:

*Esta mesa es marrón, pero ésa es azul.*

This table is brown but that one is blue.

*Aquellos niños son muy altos; éstos son bajos.*

Those children are very tall; those ones are short.

*Esto no tiene sentido.*

This doesn't make any sense.

(vii) The accents also help to distinguish between some monosyllabic words. The more emphatic words carry the accent.

| | | | | | |
|---|---|---|---|---|---|
| *dé* | (give) | ← → | *de* | (of, from) | |
| *él* | (he, him) | | *el* | (the) | |
| *más* | (more, most) | | *mas* | (but) | |
| *mí* | (me) | | *mi* | (my) | |
| *sé* | (I know) | | *se* | (himself, herself, etc.) | |
| *sí* | (yes, indeed) | | *si* | (if, whether) | |
| *té* | (tea) | | *te* | (you, yourself) | |
| *tú* | (you) | | *tu* | (your) | |

(viii) And, last but not the least, we have the case of "porque". The accent marks the difference between the question and the reason. That is,

    *por qué*   →   why
    *porque*   →   because

# 5
# NUMBERS
## *NÚMEROS*

## CARDINAL NUMBERS

| 0  | Zero      | *Cero*       |
|----|-----------|--------------|
| 1  | One       | *Uno*        |
| 2  | Two       | *Dos*        |
| 3  | Three     | *Tres*       |
| 4  | Four      | *Cuatro*     |
| 5  | Five      | *Cinco*      |
| 6  | Six       | *Seis*       |
| 7  | Seven     | *Siete*      |
| 8  | Eight     | *Ocho*       |
| 9  | Nine      | *Nueve*      |
| 10 | Ten       | *Diez*       |
| 11 | Eleven    | *Once*       |
| 12 | Twelve    | *Doce*       |
| 13 | Thirteen  | *Trece*      |
| 14 | Fourteen  | *Catorce*    |
| 15 | Fifteen   | *Quince*     |
| 16 | Sixteen   | *Dieciséis*  |
| 17 | Seventeen | *Diecisiete* |

| | | |
|---|---|---|
| 18 | Eighteen | *Dieciocho* |
| 19 | Nineteen | *Diecinueve* |
| 20 | Twenty | *Veinte* |
| 21 | Twenty-one | *Veintiuno* |
| 22 | Twenty-two | *Veintidós* |
| 23 | Twenty-three | *Veintitrés* |
| 24 | Twenty-four | *Veinticuatro* |
| 25 | Twenty-five | *Veinticinco* |
| 26 | Twenty-six | *Veintiséis* |
| 27 | Twenty-seven | *Veintisiete* |
| 28 | Twenty-eight | *Veintiocho* |
| 29 | Twenty-nine | *Veintinueve* |
| 30 | Thirty | *Treinta* |
| 31 | Thirty-one | *Treinta y uno* |
| 32 | Thirty-two | *Treinta y dos* |
| 33 | Thirty-three | *Treinta y tres* |
| 34 | Thirty-four | *Treinta y cuatro* |
| 35 | Thirty-five | *Treinta y cinco* |
| 36 | Thirty-six | *Treinta y seis* |
| 37 | Thirty-seven | *Treinta y siete* |
| 38 | Thirty-eight | *Treinta y ocho* |
| 39 | Thirty-nine | *Treinta y nueve* |
| 40 | Forty | *Cuarenta* |
| 41 | Forty-one | *Cuarenta y uno* |
| 42 | Forty-two | *Cuarenta y dos* |
| 43 | Forty-three | *Cuarenta y tres* |
| 44 | Forty-four | *Cuarenta y cuatro* |

| | | |
|---|---|---|
| 45 | Forty-five | *Cuarenta y cinco* |
| 46 | Forty-six | *Cuarenta y seis* |
| 47 | Forty-seven | *Cuarenta y siete* |
| 48 | Forty-eight | *Cuarenta y ocho* |
| 49 | Forty-nine | *Cuarenta y nueve* |
| 50 | Fifty | *Cincuenta* |
| 51 | Fifty-one | *Cincuenta y uno* |
| 52 | Fifty-two | *Cincuenta y dos* |
| 53 | Fifty-three | *Cincuenta y tres* |
| 54 | Fifty-four | *Cincuenta y cuatro* |
| 55 | Fifty-five | *Cincuenta y cinco* |
| 56 | Fifty-six | *Cincuenta y seis* |
| 57 | Fifty-seven | *Cincuenta y siete* |
| 58 | Fifty-eight | *Cincuenta y ocho* |
| 59 | Fifty-nine | *Cincuenta y nueve* |
| 60 | Sixty | *Sesenta* |
| 61 | Sixty-one | *Sesenta y uno* |
| 62 | Sixty-two | *Sesenta y dos* |
| 63 | Sixty-three | *Sesenta y tres* |
| 64 | Sixty-four | *Sesenta y cuatro* |
| 65 | Sixty-five | *Sesenta y cinco* |
| 66 | Sixty-six | *Sesenta y seis* |
| 67 | Sixty-seven | *Sesenta y siete* |
| 68 | Sixty-eight | *Sesenta y ocho* |
| 69 | Sixty-nine | *Sesenta y nueve* |
| 70 | Seventy | *Setenta* |
| 71 | Seventy-one | *Setenta y uno* |

| | | |
|---|---|---|
| 72 | Seventy-two | *Setenta y dos* |
| 73 | Seventy-three | *Setenta y tres* |
| 74 | Seventy-four | *Setenta y cuatro* |
| 75 | Seventy-five | *Setenta y cinco* |
| 76 | Seventy-six | *Setenta y seis* |
| 77 | Seventy-seven | *Setenta y siete* |
| 78 | Seventy-eight | *Setenta y ocho* |
| 79 | Seventy-nine | *Setenta y nueve* |
| 80 | Eighty | *Ochenta* |
| 81 | Eighty-one | *Ochenta y uno* |
| 82 | Eighty-two | *Ochenta y dos* |
| 83 | Eighty-three | *Ochenta y tres* |
| 84 | Eighty-four | *Ochenta y cuatro* |
| 85 | Eighty-five | *Ochenta y cinco* |
| 86 | Eighty-six | *Ochenta y seis* |
| 87 | Eighty-seven | *Ochenta y siete* |
| 88 | Eighty-eight | *Ochenta y ocho* |
| 89 | Eighty-nine | *Ochenta y nueve* |
| 90 | Ninety | *Noventa* |
| 91 | Ninety-one | *Noventa y uno* |
| 92 | Ninety-two | *Noventa y dos* |
| 93 | Ninety-three | *Noventa y tres* |
| 94 | Ninety-four | *Noventa y cuatro* |
| 95 | Ninety-five | *Noventa y cinco* |
| 96 | Ninety-six | *Noventa y seis* |
| 97 | Ninety-seven | *Noventa y siete* |
| 98 | Ninety-eight | *Noventa y ocho* |

| | | |
|---|---|---|
| 99 | Ninety-nine | *Noventa y nueve* |
| 100 | Hundred | *Cien* |
| 200 | Two hundred | *Doscient@s* |
| 300 | Three hundred | *Trescient@s* |
| 400 | Four hundred | *Cuatrocient@s* |
| 500 | Five Hundred | *Quinient@s* |
| 1000 | One thousand | *Mil* |
| 2000 | Two thousand | *Dos mil* |
| 1000,000 | One million | *Un millón* |
| 2000,000 | Two million | *Dos millones* |
| 1000,000,000 | One billion | *Mil millones* |

## To be Noted

* The hundreds take a -s at the end to denote that it is plural, for example:

100 ciento (In this case, the last syllable is lost and it's pronounced *"cien"*)

200 doscientos

300 trescientos

* 500 is an exception; it is called **qui**nientos

## ORDINAL NUMBERS

| | | |
|---|---|---|
| 1st | First | *Primer@* |
| 2nd | Second | *Segund@* |
| 3rd | Third | *Tercer@* |
| 4th | Fourth | *Cuart@* |
| 5th | Fifth | *Quint@* |
| 6th | Sixth | *Sext@* |

| 7th | Seventh | *Séptim@* |
|-----|---------|-----------|
| 8th | Eighth | *Octav@* |
| 9th | Ninth | *Noven@* |
| 10th | Tenth | *Décim@* |

## FRACTIONS

| 1/2 | a half | *la mitad* |
|------|--------|-----------|
| | | *(un medio)* |
| 1/4 | one-fourth | *un cuarto* |
| 1/3 | one-third | *un tercio* |
| 2/3 | two-thirds | *dos tercios* |
| 3/4 | three-fourth | *tres cuartos* |
| 1/6 | one-sixth | *un sexto* |
| 1/12 | one-twelfth | *un duodécimo, un dozavo* |
| 7/12 | seven-twelfths | *siete dozavos* |
| 1/100 | one-hundredth | *un centésimo* |
| 1/1000 | one-thousandth | *un milésimo* |

It is interesting to note that while mentioning centuries in Spanish, we use a cardinal number placed after the noun.

For *example*:

The twentieth century  *el siglo veinte*

# 6
# YOU
## TÚ y USTED

Like several other languages, Spanish has two sets of pronouns which can be used to address other people, all of which mean "**you**". It has the formal and the informal "you" and the singular and plural "you".

1.  Tú          Singular informal – familiar
2.  Vosotros    Plural informal
3.  Usted       Singular formal
4.  Ustedes     Plural formal

While there are exceptions, it must be kept in mind that in general, the familiar or the informal form is used for friends and family members. We can say that it can be used in the same circumstances where we use a person's first name in English.

More specifically, we can say that "you" in the familiar form is used in the following cases:

— when speaking to family members
— when speaking to friends
— when speaking to pets
— when speaking to children

— when speaking to people who start addressing you as "tú" (but if the person who starts addressing you as "tú" is someone in a position of authority over you, you should not respond in the familiar form).

— when speaking to someone who asks you to address him/her in familiar terms ("tutear").

The formal form is used in situations other than those mentioned above. It is interesting to know that in most of Latin America, the use of "tú" and "vosotros" has been replaced by the formal terms.

For *example*:

Spain: *¿Venís esta noche?* (vosotros)

Venezuela: *¿Vienen esta noche?* (ustedes)

Are you coming tonight?

## HOW ARE YOU?

¿Cómo está (**usted**)? * → *Formal singular*

¿Cómo están (**ustedes**)? → *Formal plural*

¿Cómo estás (**tú**)? → *Informal singular*

¿Cómo estáis (**vosotros**)? → *Informal plural (only in Spain)*

* In Spanish, the pronoun is normally omitted because the endings of the verbs show the person. *Usted* is always conjugated in the singular third person (as *él, ella*). When talking about conjugation, *ustedes* is like *ell@s*.

# 7
# ARTICLES
## *ARTÍCULOS*

## INDEFINITE ARTICLES

A noun is a word which represents a person, place, thing or idea.

> Person: Robert, boy, scientist
> Place: Venice, school, theatre
> Thing: table, watch, sandwich
> Idea: liberty, hatred, love

In Spanish, all nouns have a gender; they are either masculine or feminine.

The nouns that end in **-o** are usually masculine and the nouns that end in **-a** are usually feminine. The articles change according to the gender of the noun.

In Spanish, there are four indefinite articles:

| | |
|---|---|
| *UN* | masculine singular |
| *UNOS* | masculine plural |
| *UNA* | feminine singular |
| *UNAS* | feminine plural |

*UN* and *UNA* can be translated as **a** or **an** in English.

**Examples:**

| | |
|---|---|
| un libro | a book |
| un bolígrafo | a ballpoint pen |
| un lápiz | a pencil |
| una mesa | a table |
| una puerta | a door |
| una silla | a chair |
| un reloj | a clock |
| un pájaro | a bird |
| una regla | a ruler (for measuring) |
| una goma de borrar | an eraser |
| un despacho | an office |
| un sacapuntas | a sharpener |
| un coche | a car |
| una flor | a flower |
| un periódico | a newspaper |
| una radio | a radio |
| un televisor | a television set |
| una película | a film |

UNOS and UNAS can be translated either as **some** or can be left untranslated. They are normally used in a sentence before the nouns, in the plural form, which are specific. They are also used for the nouns which are in pairs.

| | |
|---|---|
| unos chicos | boys |
| unas chicas | girls |
| unos hombres | men |

| *unas mujeres* | women |
| *unos huevos* | eggs |

## EXPRESSIONS

*¿Qué es esto?*

What is this?

*(Esto) Es un reloj.*

This is a clock.

*(Esto) Es un sillón.*

This is an armchair.

*(Esto) Son sillones.*

These are armchairs.

*¿Quién es?*

Who is this?

*(Esta) Es una chica.*

This is a girl.

*(Este) Es un chico.*

This is a boy.

*(Estos) son sus padres.*

These are his parents.

In Spanish, the masculine forms end with **-o** in most of the cases and change to **-a** in the feminine form. Thus the sign @ denotes that to change the masculine form to the feminine form, simply change the **-o** at the end to **-a**.

For *example*, l@s amig@s (the friends) denotes:

| *los amigos* | → | the friends (masculine) |
| *las amigas* | → | the friends (feminine). |

# DEFINITE ARTICLES

In Spanish, there are four definite articles.

| | |
|---|---|
| EL | masculine singular |
| LOS | masculine plural |
| LA | feminine singular |
| LAS | feminine plural |

All the four definite articles can be translated as *the* in English.

*Examples*:

| | |
|---|---|
| *la calculadora* | the calculator |
| *el estuche* | the pencil-case |
| *el bolígrafo* | the ballpoint pen |
| *el rotulador* | the felt tip pen |
| *el ordenador* | the computer |
| *el lector de CDs* | the CD player |
| *el cuaderno* | the notebook |
| *la agenda* | the diary |
| *la caja* | the box |
| *l@s amig@s* | the friends |
| *las camas* | the beds |
| *las lámparas* | the lamps |
| *el hermano* | the brother |
| *el animal* | the animal |
| *el color* | the colour |
| *la música* | the music |

# PLURAL

In Spanish, plurals are typically formed by adding -s or **-es** to a word **(adjectives have also a gender and number).** There are a few easy rules that must be considered.

1. If a word ends with a vowel, simply add –s.

   el perro → los perro**s**        the dogs
   la casa → las casa**s**          the houses

2. If a word ends with a consonant, simply add –**es.**

   el árbol → los árbol**es**        the trees
   la flor → las flor**es**          the flowers

3. If a word ends with -z, change it to –c before adding –**es.**

   el lápiz → los lápi**ces**        the pencils
   feliz → feli**ces**               happy

4. If a word ends with –**ón,** drop the accent and add –**es.**

   el avión → los avi**ones**        the planes
   la canción → las canci**ones**    the songs

5. If a plural refers to a mixed group, use the masculine plural.

   el gato + la gata → los gat**os**   the cats
   *but, dos gatas (two female cats)* →*las gatas*

6. Some compound nouns form their plural by changing only the article.

   **el** paraguas → **los** paraguas        the umbrellas

# 8
# CONTRACTED ARTICLES
## *CONTRACCIONES*

As the name suggests, the definite articles and the prepositions **A** and **DE** contract to form the contracted articles.

The preposition **A** means "to / at / in" in Spanish.

*Examples*:

> He goes to Paris.
> *Va **a** Paris.*

We have already studied the definite articles.

| | |
|---|---|
| *el* | masculine singular |
| *la* | feminine singular |
| *los* | masculine plural |
| *las* | feminine plural |

which mean 'The'.

The preposition **A** and the definite article "el" contract in the following manner to form contracted articles:

$$A + el \rightarrow al$$

The other forms don't change :

$$A + la \rightarrow a\ la$$
$$A + los \rightarrow a\ los$$
$$A + las \rightarrow a\ las$$

These can be translated as 'to the', 'at the' or 'in the'.

*Examples:*

She goes to the airport.
*Ella va (a + el) al aeropuerto.*

He goes to the station.
*Él va (a + la) a la estación.*

We go to the market.
*Nosotros vamos (a + el) al mercado.*

They go to school.
*Ellos van (a + la) a la escuela.*

Similarly, the preposition **DE** means 'of' or 'from'.

*Examples:*

He is coming from Milan.
*Viene de Milan.*

She is coming from London.
*Viene de London.*

The preposition *DE* and the definite article "el" contract in the following manner to form contracted articles:

$$De + el \rightarrow del$$

But the other forms don't change :

De + la → de la

De + los → de los

De + las → de las

That can be translated as 'of the' or 'from the'.

*Examples*:

I have come from the market.
*Yo He venido del mercado.*

Have you come from the cinema?
*¿Has venido del cine?.*

We are coming from the shops.
*Venimos de las tiendas.*

The colour of the shirt is beautiful.
*El color de la camiseta es bonito.*

# 9
# DAYS AND MONTHS
## *LOS DÍAS y LOS MESES*

## DAYS OF THE WEEK
*Días de la semana*

| | |
|---|---|
| Monday | *lunes* |
| Tuesday | *martes* |
| Wednesday | *miércoles* |
| Thursday | *jueves* |
| Friday | *viernes* |
| Saturday | *sábado* |
| Sunday | *domingo* |

The days of a week in Spanish start with a small letter and are preceded by a definite article **el**. For example el lunes.

## MONTHS OF THE YEAR
*Meses del año*

| | |
|---|---|
| January | *enero* |
| February | *febrero* |
| March | *marzo* |
| April | *abril* |
| May | *mayo* |

| June | *junio* |
|------|---------|
| July | *julio* |
| August | *agosto* |
| September | *septiembre* |
| October | *octubre* |
| November | *noviembre* |
| December | *diciembre* |

The months in Spanish also start with a small letter. To refer to a month, use the preposition *EN* or write *En el mes de.*

## ASKING FOR THE DAY AND MONTH

What day is it today?
*¿Qué día es hoy?*

Today is Monday.
*Hoy es lunes.*

Which month is this?
*¿A qué mes estamos?*

It is June.
*Estamos en junio.*

In January
*En Enero*

In the month of January
*En el mes de enero*

# 10
# DATE AND TIME
## *LA FECHA y LA HORA*

## TIME
## *La hora*

### VOCABULARY

| | |
|---|---|
| a watch | *un reloj (de pulsera)* |
| a clock | *un reloj (de pared)* |
| a hand | *una aguja* |
| the minute hand | *el minutero* |
| the second hand | *el segundero* |
| the hour hand | *el horario* |
| numbers | *los números* |
| a dial | *una esfera* |
| an hour | *una hora* |
| a minute | *un minuto* |
| a second | *un segundo* |
| a quarter | *un cuarto* |
| morning | *la mañana* |
| afternoon | *la tarde* |
| evening | *la tarde* |
| night | *la noche* |
| sun | *el sol* |

( 36 )

| moon | la luna |
| stars | las estrellas |
| the sky | el cielo |
| clouds | las nubes |

## EXPRESSIONS

What is the time?
*¿Qué hora es?*

At what time?
*¿A qué hora?*

late
*con retraso*

before time
*con adelanto (antes de tiempo)*

| 24:00/00:00 | It is midnight | *Es medianoche* |
| 01:00 | It is 1 o'clock | *\*Es la una (de la madrugada)* |
| 02:00 | It is 2 o'clock | *Son las dos* |
| 03:00 | It is 3 o'clock | *Son las tres* |
| 12:00 | It is noon | *Son las doce* |
| 13:00 | It is 1 p.m. | *\*Es la una (de la tarde)* |
| 15:00 | It is 3 p.m. | *Son las tres (de la tarde)* |
| 06:30 | It is six thirty | *Son las seis y treinta* |
| | It is half past six | *Son las seis y media* |

\* *Es la* is used only for one o'clock.

( 37 )

| | | |
|---|---|---|
| 06:15 | It is six fifteen | *Son las seis y quince* |
| | It is quarter past six | *Son las seis y cuarto* |
| 06:45 | It is six forty-five | *Son las seis y cuarenta y cinco* |
| | It is quarter to seven | *Son las siete menos cuarto* |
| 06:10 | It is ten past six | *Son las seis y diez* |
| 06:50 | It is six fifty | *Son las seis cincuenta* |
| | It is ten to seven | *Son las siete menos diez* |

## DATE
## *La Fecha*

## VOCABULARY

| | |
|---|---|
| A day | *un día* |
| A week | *una semana* |
| A fortnight | *una quincena* |
| A month | *un mes* |
| A year | *un año* |
| The day before yesterday | *anteayer* |
| Yesterday | *ayer* |
| Today | *hoy* |
| Tomorrow | *mañana* |
| The day after tomorrow | *pasado mañana* |
| Last week | *la semana pasada* |
| Next week | *la semana próxima / la semana que viene* |

| Last month | *el mes pasado* |
|---|---|
| Next month | *el mes próximo / el mes que viene* |
| Last year | *el año pasado* |
| Next year | *el año próximo / el año que viene* |

In Spanish the date is preceded by the definite article **el**. So, to write a date, use –

> el + the number + the month.
> *El 7 de junio de 2007*

But if the day is also mentioned, one can omit the article –

> *Jueves 7 de junio de 2007*

> What is the date today?
> *¿Qué día es hoy?*

This question can be answered in two ways.

> *Hoy estamos a 27 de marzo de 2007.*
> *Hoy es veintisiete de marzo de 2007.*

To refer to a year, use the preposition *EN*

> In 1848
> *En 1848*

**Note:** In the morning I go to school.

> *Por la mañana voy a la escuela.*

I go to school at 8 in the morning.

> *Voy a la escuela a las ocho de la mañana.*

In a general statement, we use **por** but with reference to time we use **de** to say "in the morning", "in the afternoon" or "in the evening".

# 11
# THE COLOURS
## *LOS COLORES*

Of which colour is...?
*¿De qué color es...?*

|  | **Singular** | **Plural** |
|---|---|---|
| Red | *Roj@* | *Roj@s* |
| Blue | *Azul* | *Azules* |
| Green | *Verde* | *Verdes* |
| Yellow | *Amarill@* | *Amarill@s* |
| Orange | *Naranja* | *Naranjas* |
| Violet | *Violeta* | *Violetas* |
| White | *Blanc@* | *Blanc@s* |
| Black | *Negr@* | *Negr@s* |
| Grey | *Gris* | *Grises* |
| Brown | *Marrón* | *Marrones* |
| Pink | *Rosa* | *Rosas* |
| Deep red | *Burdeos* | *Burdeos* |
| Sky blue | *Azul celeste* | *Azul celeste* |
| Light blue | *Azul claro* | *Azul claro* |
| Dark blue | *Azul oscuro* | *Azul oscuro* |
| Turquoise | *Turquesa* | *Turquesa* |

Unlike English, the colours in Spanish change to agree to the gender and number of the noun (*rosa*, *gris*, *naranja*, *burdeos* and *turquesa* don't change to agree to the gender).

Using the modifiers, dark (*oscuro*) and light (*claro*), make the colour invariable, that is, it does not change to agree to the number or gender.

The colours are always placed after the noun.

*For example,*

a green book
*un libro verde*

# 12
# VERBS
## LOS VERBOS

There are three groups of verbs in Spanish which are determined by the endings of the verbs. But before classifying these verbs we need to see their infinitive form, from which we derive their conjugated form. The verbs in the infinitive form are called so because they are not bound by time. The infinitive form in English is preceded by the word 'to'.

| | |
|---|---|
| to sing | *cantar* |
| to eat | *comer* |
| to leave | *partir* |

We conjugate these verbs in accordance with time, that is, in the present, past or the future tense.

All regular verbs can be divided into three groups based on the ending, that is, the last two letters of the verb. The first group consists of verbs ending in **-ar**; the second group consists of verbs ending in **-er** and the third group consist of has those ending in **-ir**. Verbs are generally conjugated in six forms according to the person(s)/subject(s).

1. yo               I
2. tú             You (singular and informal)

| 3. | él | He |
|---|---|---|
| | ella | She |
| | usted | You (singular and formal) |
| 4. | nosotr@s | We |
| 5. | vosotr@s | You (plural and informal) |
| 6. | ell@s | They |
| | ustedes | You (plural and formal) |

The conjugation in the *él* and *ella* forms and in the *ellos* and *ellas* forms is always the same. You use them depending on the gender. If you're referring to a group where there are both masculine and feminine elements, you must use *ellos*. Don't forget that, unlike English, in Spanish the formal terms *usted* y *ustedes* are conjugated in the same way as the third person. For example:

To sing:

él can**ta** (he sings)  → usted can**ta** (you sing)
ellos can**tan** (they sing) → ustedes can**tan** (you sing)

The main difference that appears, if you compare the Spanish and the English personal pronoun system is that, in Spanish, pronouns **do not need to be expressed** since the verb itself identifies the subject.

I want to visit Madrid. → (yo) *Quiero visitar Madrid.*

However, it is obligatory to mention the pronoun if there is a risk of confusion. This case is frequently used in the **Imperfecto forms (see lesson 25)**. For example, *"solía visitar la ciudad"* can be translated in three ways:

I used to visit the city.

→ YO solía visitar la ciudad.

He/She used to visit the city.

→ ÉL/ELLA solía visitar la ciudad.

You (formal) used to visit the city.

→ USTED solía visitar la ciudad.

## VERBS

To memorise the conjugation of a verb, you only need to memorise the endings because the stem of the verb normally remains the same. To form the present indicative of regular verbs, drop the infinitive ending (**-ar**, **-er**, or **-ir**) and add the endings below.

For example, the verb 'Hablar' is in the infinitive form, **-ar** is the ending of the verb and the beginning 'Habl' is the stem. The endings of **-ar** verbs are as follows:

### Hablar (To speak)

| Yo | o | hablo | I speak |
|----|-----|--------|-----------|
| Tú | as | hablas | You speak |
| Él | a | habla | He speaks |
| Ella | a | habla | She speaks |
| Nosotr@s | amos | hablamos | We speak |
| Vosotr@s | áis | habláis | You speak |
| Ell@s | an | hablan | They speak |

### Cantar (To sing)

| | | |
|----|----|----|
| Yo canto | | I sing |
| Tú cantas | | You sing |
| Él canta | | He sings |

| *Ella canta* | She sings |
|---|---|
| *Nosotr@s cantamos* | We sing |
| *Vosotr@s cantáis* | You sing |
| *Ell@s cantan* | They sing |

Sometimes the **-ar** verbs undergo a change to facilitate the pronunciation.

The second group of verbs are those that end in **-er**. For example, *comer* (to eat), *beber* (to drink), etc. They take the following endings:

**Comer** (To eat)

| *Yo* | **o** | *como* | I eat |
|---|---|---|---|
| *Tú* | **es** | *comes* | You eat |
| *Él* | **e** | *come* | He eats |
| *Ella* | **e** | *come* | She eats |
| *Nosotr@s* | **emos** | *comemos* | We eat |
| *Vosotr@s* | **éis** | *coméis* | You eat |
| *Ell@s* | **en** | *comen* | They eat |

**Beber** (To drink)

| *Yo bebo* | I drink |
|---|---|
| *Tú bebes* | You drink |
| *Él bebe* | He drinks |
| *Ella bebe* | She drinks |
| *Nosotr@s bebemos* | We drink |
| *Vosotr@s bebéis* | You drink |
| *Ell@s beben* | They drink |

The third group of verbs are those that end in **-ir**. For example, *abrir* (to open), *recibir* (to receive).

These verbs take the following endings with them:

**Abrir** (To open)

| Yo | o | abro | I open |
|----|----|----|----|
| Tú | es | abres | You open |
| Él | e | abre | He opens |
| Ella | e | abre | She opens |
| Nosotr@s | imos | abrimos | We open |
| Vosotr@s | ís | abrís | You open |
| Ell@s | en | abren | They open |

**Recibir** (To receive)

| Yo recibo | I receive |
|----|----|
| Tú recibes | You receive |
| Él recibe | He receives |
| Ella recibe | She receives |
| Nosotr@s recibimos | We receive |
| Vosotr@s recibís | You receive |
| Ell@s reciben | They receive |

**There are other irregular verbs whose conjugations are very important.**

**SER** (To be)

| Yo soy | I am |
|----|----|
| Tú eres | You are |
| Él es | He is |
| Ella es | She is |
| Nosotr@s somos | We are |
| Vosotr@s sois | You are |
| Ell@s son | They are |

## TENER (To have)

| | |
|---|---|
| Yo tengo | I have |
| Tú tienes | You have |
| Él tiene | He has |
| Ella tiene | She has |
| Nosotr@s tenemos | We have |
| Vosotr@s tenéis | You have |
| Ell@s tienen | They have |

## HABER (To have, auxiliary)

| | |
|---|---|
| Yo he | I have |
| Tú has | You have |
| Él ha | He has |
| Ella ha | She has |
| Nosotr@s hemos | We have |
| Vosotr@s habéis | You have |
| Ell@s han | They have |

## IR (To go)

| | |
|---|---|
| Yo voy | I go |
| Tú vas | You go |
| Él va | He goes |
| Ella va | She goes |
| Nosotr@s vamos | We go |
| Vosotr@s vais | You go |
| Ell@s van | They go |

## VENIR (To come)

| | |
|---|---|
| Yo vengo | I come |
| Tú vienes | You come |
| Él viene | He comes |
| Ella viene | She comes |
| Nosotr@s venimos | We come |
| Vosotr@s venís | You come |
| Ell@s vienen | They come |

## HACER (To do/To make)

| | |
|---|---|
| Yo hago | I do/make |
| Tú haces | You do/make |
| Él hace | He does/makes |
| Ella hace | She does/makes |
| Nosotr@s hacemos | We do/make |
| Vosotr@s hacéis | You do/make |
| Ell@s hacen | They do/make |

## PODER (To be able to)

| | |
|---|---|
| Yo puedo | I can |
| Tú puedes | You can |
| Él puede | He can |
| Ella puede | She can |
| Nosotr@s podemos | We can |
| Vosotr@s podéis | You can |
| Ell@s pueden | They can |

## QUERER (To want)

| | |
|---|---|
| *Yo quiero* | I want |
| *Tú quieres* | You want |
| *Él quiere* | He wants |
| *Ella quiere* | She wants |
| *Nosotr@s queremos* | We want |
| *Vosotr@s queréis* | You want |
| *Ell@s quieren* | They want |

## PONER (To put)

| | |
|---|---|
| *Yo pongo* | I put |
| *Tú pones* | You put |
| *Él pone* | He puts |
| *Ella pone* | She puts |
| *Nosotr@s ponemos* | We put |
| *Vosotr@s ponéis* | You put |
| *Ell@s ponen* | They put |

# 13
# TO BE
## SER y ESTAR

For an English speaker, one of the most difficult things to master is the use of *ser* and *estar*. *Ser* and *estar* can both be translated as "*to be*" (I am, you are, etc.) but depending on what you are saying, you will have to decide which one of them to use because they have very specific meanings and are not interchangeable.

Notice that the sentence "*the apple is green*" can have different meanings in English: perhaps the apple is not ripe, but it can also express that the colour of the apple is green. In Spanish, a different verb is used to express "to be" depending on whether the speaker intends to address a condition ("*estar*") or an essential quality ("*ser*"). For example:

- *La manzana ES (ser) verde*. Here, "verde" means green colour; it is an essential quality.
- *La manzana ESTÁ (estar) verde*. Here, "Verde" means unripe; it's a condition of the apple.

So, let's see the different uses of these verbs.

**SER**

*Yo soy*

*Tú eres*

*Él/Ella es*
*Nosotr@s somos*
*Vosotr@s sois*
*Ell@s son*

Ser is an irregular verb that mainly defines and identifies, but it is also used in the following different ways:

- to identify people, professions and things:
  *Él es abogado.*
  He is a lawyer.

- to express nationality or origin:
  *Guadalupe es mejicana.*
  Guadalupe is Mexican.

- to express possession:
  *El coche es mío.*
  The car is mine.

- to tell the time and date:
  *¿Qué hora es?*
  What time is it?

- to indicate permanent personal characteristics:
  *Ana y Miguel son muy educados.*
  Ana and Miguel are very polite.

- to specify where an event will take place:
  *La conferencia es en la biblioteca.*
  The conference is in the library.

- to express opinions:
  *Es una película muy buena.*
  It is a very good film.

- to form the passive voice:
  *La casa fue incendiada.*
  The house was burned down.

## ESTAR

*Yo estoy*
*Tú estás*
*Él/Ella está*
*Nosotr@s estamos*
*Vosotr@s estáis*
*Ell@s están*

*Estar* is also an irregular verb that expresses conditions, locations and situations, such as how something looks, feels or tastes at a given moment. Let's explore some uses:

- physical welfare or condition, or state of health:
  *Sonia está enferma.*
  Sonia is ill.

- location or distance:
  *Estaba en la cocina y no escuché el teléfono.*
  I was in the kitchen and I did not hear the phone.

- personal emotional conditions:
  *Esa mujer está deprimida.*
  That woman is depressed.

- weather conditions:
  *Está lloviendo.*
  It's raining.

- continuous tenses:
  *¿Qué estás haciendo?*
  What are you doing?

- condition or state of food and things:
  *La sopa está fría.*
  The soup is cold.

- in some fixed idiomatic expressions:

| | |
|---|---|
| *estar acostumbrad@* | to be accustomed to |
| *estar content@* | to be happy |
| *estar de acuerdo* | to agree |
| *estar de buen/mal humor* | to be in a good/bad mood |
| *estar apurado* | to be in a hurry |
| *estar de vacaciones* | to be on vacation |
| *estar de vuelta* | to be back |
| *estar listo* | to be ready |
| *estar de moda* | to be in fashion |
| *estar de viaje* | to be on a trip |
| *estar embarazada* | to be pregnant |

So, in Spanish, to say *"¿Cómo estás?"* is very different from saying *"¿Cómo eres?"*. In English, both the sentences mean *"How are you?"*. But in the first case, you're being asked for your condition at the moment. In this case you should answer, for example, *"Bien, gracias"* (*"Fine, thanks"*). And in the second case, someone wants to know your general characteristics. You can say, for example, *"Soy alt@, delgad@ y sensible"* (*"I'm tall, thin and sensitive"*).

# 14
# INTERROGATIVE FORM
## LA FORMA INTERROGATIVA

In Spanish, the simplest way to form a question is to change the intonation:

En España hace calor. → ¿En España, ¿hace calor?

In Spain, it is hot. → Is it hot in Spain?

Note that the written form of Spanish warns the reader that a question or exclamation is coming up by using an inverted question or exclamation mark at the beginning of the phrase.

¿Cuántos hijos tienes?

How many children do you have?

Changes in word order are also common in formal Spanish:

Ellas estudian → ¿Estudian ellas?

They study → Do they study?

El señor Delís es de Galicia. →
¿Es de Galicia el señor Delís?

Mister Delís comes from Galicia. →
Does Mister Delís come from Galicia?

Picasso creó cuadros maravillosos. →
¿Creó Picasso cuadros maravillosos?

( 54 )

Picasso created wonderful pictures. →
Did Picasso create wonderful pictures?

Another method of forming questions is to add a
tag question to the end of a statement.

*Slater habla español, ¿no?*
Slater speaks Spanish, doesn't he?

*Slater habla español, ¿verdad?*
Slater speaks Spanish, right?

## POSSIBLE QUESTIONS IN SPANISH

In Spanish, there are some common words used for
questions. In these types of sentences, notice how the
subject and the verb are inverted. Examples:

*¿Cuándo come usted?*
When do you eat?

*¿Dónde está mi coche?*
Where is my car?

*¿Cuánto cuesta el reloj?*
How much does the clock cost?

| | |
|---|---|
| How many? | *¿Cuánt@s?* |
| How? | *¿Cómo?* |
| When? | *¿Cuándo?* |
| Which? | *¿Qué?* |
| Which one? | *¿Cuál?* |
| | *¿Cuáles?* |
| Where? | *¿Dónde?* |
| From where? | *¿De dónde?* |
| Since when? | *¿Desde cuándo?* |

| Why? | ¿Por qué? |
| Of which colour? | ¿De qué color? |
| What is the time? | ¿Qué hora es? |
| At what time? | ¿A qué hora? |
| How is the weather? | ¿Qué tiempo hace? |
| What is this? | ¿Qué es? |
| Is it that...? | ¿Es que...? |
| What? | ¿Qué? |
| Who? | ¿Quién? |
| To whom? | ¿A quién? |
| About what? | ¿Sobre qué? |
| Whose? | ¿De quién? |

## INTERROGATIVE ADJECTIVES
### Adjetivos interrogativos

The interrogative adjectives do not vary according to the gender and the number of the noun.

QUÉ is used for the singular and plural forms of both masculine and feminine genders.

Which book are you reading?
*¿Qué libro estás leyendo?*

→ masculine singular

Which T-shirt do you prefer?
*¿Qué camiseta prefieres?*

→ feminine singular

Which trousers do you like?
*¿Qué pantalones te gustan?*

→ masculine plural

Which pens do you like?

*¿Qué plumas te gustan?*

→ feminine plural

## INTERROGATIVE PRONOUNS
*Pronombres interrogativos*

The interrogative pronouns, unlike the interrogative adjectives, vary according to the number of the subject.

Cuál      singular      (masculine and feminine)

Cuáles    plural        (masculine and feminine)

We have many pens. Which one do you like?

*Tenemos muchos bolígrafos. ¿Cuál prefieres?*

We use the pronoun 'Cuál' to replace the singular noun *'qué* bolígrafo' (which pen).

There are several books in this library. Which ones have you read?

*Hay muchos libros en esta biblioteca. ¿Cuáles ha leído usted?*

We use the pronoun 'Cuáles' to replace the plural noun *'qué libros'* (which books).

When used with the verb "ser", cuál and qué can both mean "what" but they are not interchangeable. "Cuál" is more common, and is used to indicate a selection or choice of possibilities. "Qué" is used to elicit a definition or an explanation. Examples:

*¿Cuál es la capital de Argentina?*

What is the capital of Argentina?

*¿Qué es la capital?*

What is the definition of a capital?

# 15
# PREPOSITIONS
## LOS PREPOSICIONES

The various prepositions in English can be easily translated in Spanish. The Spanish prepositions are:

- **at, in — *en***

    He is at the hotel.

    *Está en el hotel.*

    He is in Tokyo.

    *Está en Tokyo.*

    The pen is in the bag.

    *El bolígrafo está en el bolso.*

- **next to, beside — *al lado de***

    She is sitting next to the boy.

    *Ella está sentada al lado del niño.*

- **after — *después de***

    I am going to come after the party.

    *Voy a venir después de la fiesta.*

- **about, on (the subject of) — *sobre, acerca de***

    The professor is speaking about/on politics.

    *El profesor habla acerca de política.*

- **before** — *antes de*

    The girl will eat before coming.
    *La chica comerá antes de venir.*

- **with** — *con*

    He always goes to the pool with his wife.
    *Siempre va a la piscina con su mujer.*

- **against** — *contra*

    Everyone is against me.
    *Todos están contra mí.*

- **according to** — *según*

    According to Peter, one must not smoke.
    *Según Peter, no se debe fumar.*

- **from, of, about** — *de*

    He comes from Delhi.
    *Es de Delhi.*

    The bag is made of cloth.
    *El bolso está hecho de tela.*

    He speaks about the party.
    *Él habla de la fiesta.*

- **since** — *desde*

    He has been working in the university since 1956.
    *Trabaja en la universidad desde 1956.*

- **for** — *desde hace*

    He has been working in the office for 5 years.
    *Trabaja en la oficina desde hace cinco años.*

- **behind** — *detrás de*

  The garden is behind the house.
  *El jardín está detrás de la casa.*

- **in front of** — *delante de*

  The car is in front of the house.
  *El coche está delante de la casa.*

- **during** — *durante*

  It rained during the night.
  *Ha llovido durante la noche.*

- **while** — *mientras*

  He taught while I was learning the lesson.
  *Dio clase mientras yo aprendía la lecciün.*

- **outside** — *fuera de*

  The dog stays outside the room.
  *El perro se queda fuera de la habitación.*

  He stays outside the town.
  *Vive fuera de la ciudad.*

- **opposite to, in front of** — *enfrente de*

  The hospital is opposite to/in front of my villa.
  *El hospital está enfrente de mi chalé.*

- **between** — *entre*

  Sit between those two boys.
  *Siéntese usted entre esos dos chicos.*

- **towards** — *hacia*

  His attitude towards his mother is not good.
  *Su comportamiento hacia su madre no es bueno.*

- **until, up to — *hasta***

  The children stay in this school up to the age of five years.

  *Los niños permanecen en esta escuela hasta los cinco años.*

- **despite — *a pesar de***

  He went out despite the bad weather.

  *Salió a pesar del mal tiempo.*

- **by, through — *por***

  I saw something through the window.

  *Vi algo por la ventana.*

  The party was organized by Yago Fernández.

  *La fiesta fue organizada por Yago Fernández.*

- **among — *entre***

  He chose this house among the others.

  *Eligió esta casa entre las otras.*

- **for — *para***

  I study for the exam.

  *Estudio para el examen.*

- **near — *cerca de***

  The table is near the door.

  *La mesa está cerca de la puerta.*

- **without — *sin***

  I won't leave without him.

  *No me voy sin él.*

- **under** — *bajo*

    The cat is under the bed.

    *El gato está bajo la cama.*

- **on** — *sobre*

    The book is on the table.

    *El libro está sobre la mesa.*

# 16
# NEGATION
## LA NEGACIÓN

Look at the following sentences:

| | | |
|---|---|---|
| I eat. | → | I don't eat. |
| *Como.* | → | *No como.* |
| He is tall. | → | He is not tall. |
| *Es alto.* | → | *No es alto.* |
| Ana lives in Madrid. | → | She doesn't live in Paris. |
| *Ana vive en Madrid.* | → | *No vive en París.* |

We have learnt how to make simple affirmative statements. To make a statement negative, simply place **no** before the verb. Examples:

*Paquito es cantante.*
Paquito is a singer.

*Paquito no es cantante.*
Paquito is not a singer.

If you are answering a question in negative, two negative particles must be added. Examples:

| | |
|---|---|
| *¿Tienes otro examen?* | *No, no tengo exámenes hoy.* |
| Do you have another exam? | No, I don't have any exam today. |

In Spanish, there are several negative words used frequently. They can be used alone, preceding the verb. See the following pairs of words:

*algo* (something)  → *nada* (nothing)

*alguien* (somebody)  → *nadie* (nobody)

*algún* (-o, -a, -os, -a) (some, something)
→ *ningún* (-o, -a, -os, -as) (no, none)

*siempre* (always)  → *nunca* (never)

*también* (also)  → *tampoco* (neither)

Let's see some examples:

**Nada** *es imposible.*

**Nothing** is impossible.

**Nadie** *quiere irse.*

**Nobody** wants to leave.

**Ninguna** *ciudad es más bonita que la mía.*

**No** city is more beautiful than mine.

**Nunca** *te veo.*

I **never** see you.

But a negative (normally *no*) is always used before the verb if any one of the negative words given above is placed after the verb. Double negatives are acceptable in Spanish.

*No habla* **nadie**.

Nobody speaks.

*Él no bebe* **nunca** *alcohol.*

He never drinks alcohol.

Spanish also has other negative forms like:

*ya no* (no longer)

> I no longer eat tomatoes.
> 
> ***Ya no** como tomates.*

*todavía no* (not yet)

> I have not yet finished the work.
> 
> ***Todavía no** he terminado el trabajo.*

*no... en absoluto* (not at all)

> I am not at all thirsty.
> 
> *No tengo sed **en absoluto**.*

*no... siquiera* (none)

> I have no idea.
> 
> *No tengo **siquiera** idea.*

*sólo* (only)

> He is only five years old.
> 
> ***Sólo** tiene cinco años.*

*no... ni... ni* (neither ... nor)

> I neither eat ham nor chicken.
> 
> *No como **ni** jamón **ni** pollo.*

*apenas* (hardly)

> I hardly speak to Mr. García.
> 
> ***Apenas** hablo con el señor García.*

# 17
# ADJECTIVES
## *LOS ADJETIVOS*

Unlike English adjectives, in Spanish most adjectives have an ending depending upon whether the word they describe is masculine or feminine, singular or plural. The correct form of the adjective depends upon the noun it describes. Let's look at the forms of the adjective *bonito* (nice):

| | | |
|---|---|---|
| *un piano bonito* | → | *a nice piano* |
| *una casa bonita* | → | *a nice house* |
| *unos dibujos bonitos* | → | *nice pictures* |
| *unas esculturas bonitas* | → | *nice sculptures* |

If an adjective ends with **–e**, then it only has two forms: singular and plural. Let's see an example. *Amable* (kind*)*:

| | | |
|---|---|---|
| *una chica amable* | → | *a kind girl* |
| *unos chicos amables* | → | *kind boys* |

Similarly most adjectives that end with a consonant **do** change form for singular or plural, but **do not** change for masculine or feminine. To form the plural of such adjectives, add "**–es**".

In Spanish, it is very important to know that adjectives are normally placed **after the noun** they describe.

## VOCABULARY

| | |
|---|---|
| poor | *pobre* |
| attractive | *atractiv@* |
| famous | *famos@* |
| comfortable | *cómod@* |
| modest | *modest@* |
| alone | *sol@* |
| annoying | *molest@* |
| thankful | *agradecid@* |
| honest | *sincer@* |
| economic | *económic@* |
| charming | *encantador, encantadora* |
| cool | *fresc@* |
| active | *activ@* |
| simple | *sencill@* |
| lonely | *solitari@* |
| serious | *seri@* |
| first class | *primera clase* |
| fair | *just@* |
| wrong | *equivocad@* |
| fat | *gord@* |
| dumb (silly) | *tont@* |
| thin | *delgad@* |
| fantastic | *fantástic@* |
| lazy | *perezos@* |
| kind | *amable* |

| | |
|---|---|
| happy | *feliz* |
| unhappy | *infeliz* |
| educated | *cult@* |
| patient | *paciente* |
| dangerous | *peligros@* |
| rude | *groser@* |
| fatty | *gras@* |
| big | *grande* |
| good | *buen@* |
| hard | *dur@* |
| ugly | *fe@* |
| hot | *caliente* |
| wonderful | *maravillos@* |
| safe | *segur@* |
| late | *tardí@* |
| brilliant | *brillante* |
| closed | *cerrad@* |
| healthy | *saludable* |
| sweet | *dulce* |
| expensive | *car@* |
| dead | *muert@* |
| high | *alt@* |
| handsome | *guap@* |
| hungry | *hambrient@* |
| smart | *elegante* |
| interesting | *interesante* |
| young | *joven* |
| complicated | *complicad@* |
| sick | *enferm@* |

| | |
|---|---|
| wet/humid | *húmed@* |
| nervous | *nervios@* |
| pretty | *bonit@* |
| creative | *creativ@* |
| critical | *crític@* |
| long | *larg@* |
| slow | *lent@* |
| free | *libre* |
| pleasant | *agradable* |
| boring | *aburrid@* |
| loud | *alt@* |
| funny | *divertid@* |
| modern | *modern@* |
| fast | *rápid@* |
| beautiful | *bell@* |
| weak | *débil* |
| difficult | *difícil* |
| courageous | *valiente* |
| new | *nuev@* |
| cold | *frí@* |
| small | *pequeñ@* |
| strange | *rar@* |
| curious | *curios@* |
| short | *cort@* |
| normal | *normal* |
| open | *abiert@* |
| practical | *práctic@* |
| punctual | *puntual* |
| rich | *ric@* |

| | |
|---|---|
| calm | *tranquil@* |
| clean | *limpi@* |
| important | *importante* |
| wild | *salvaje* |
| satisfied | *satisfech@* |
| angry | *enfadad@* |
| bad | *mal@* |
| dirty | *suci@* |
| sad | *triste* |
| typical | *típic@* |
| crazy | *loc@* |
| careful | *cuidados@* |
| warm | *templad@* |
| merry (fun-loving) | *farrer@* |
| impressive | *impresionante* |
| injured | *herid@* |
| intelligent | *inteligente* |
| ignorant | *ignorante* |
| inappropriate | *improcedente* |
| decent | *decente* |
| elegant | *elegante* |
| humble | *humilde* |
| graceful | *agraciad@* |
| sturdy | *fuerte* |
| harsh | *dur@* |
| loyal | *leal* |
| desirable | *deseable* |

*Note*: Ordinal numbers are *adjectives*, and must therefore take adjective endings when they precede a noun.

# 18
# POSSESSIVE ADJECTIVES AND PRONOUNS
## *LOS ADJETIVOS y LOS PRONOMBRES POSESIVOS*

To show that an object belongs to someone, in English we use an apostrophe, but in Spanish we show the possession by using the preposition *de*.

*Example*:

This is Pedro's watch.

*Este es el reloj de Pedro.* (Literally translated as This is the watch of Pedro.)

This is Robert's house.

*Esta es la casa de Robert.* (Literally translated as This is the house of Robert.)

These are the teacher's books.

*Estos son los libros del maestro.* (Literally translated as These are the books of the teacher.)

## POSSESSIVE ADJECTIVES

*Los adjetivos posesivos*

In Spanish, the possessive adjectives change according to the number of the things possessed. The plural, first and second persons also change their gender.

|  | **Plural** | **Singular Masculine** | **Singular Feminine** | |
|---|---|---|---|---|
| *Yo* | *mis* | *mi* | *mi* | my |
| *Tú* | *tus* | *tu* | *tu* | your |
| *Él (usted)* | *sus* | *su* | *su* | his |
| *Ella* | *sus* | *su* | *su* | her |
| *Nosotr@s* | *nuestr@s* | *nuestro* | *nuestra* | our |
| *Vosotr@s* | *vuestr@s* | *vuestro* | *vuestra* | your |
| *Ell@s (ustedes)* | *sus* | *su* | *su* | their |

For *Example*:

>This is my book.
>
>*Este es mi libro.*

We put '*mi*' because the possessor is "yo" and the object possessed '*libro*' is singular.

>This is your sister.
>
>*Esta es tu hermana.*

We put '*tu*' because the possessor is "tú" and the object possessed '*hermana*' is singular.

>These are his dolls.
>
>*Estas son sus muñecas.*

We put '*sus*' because the possessor is 'él' and the object possessed '*muñecas*' is plural.

>These are your apples.
>
>*Estas son vuestras manzanas.*

We put '*vuestras*' because the possessor is 'vosotr@s' and the object possessed '*manzanas*' is feminine and plural.

# POSSESSIVE PRONOUNS
## Los pronombres posesivos

Like the possessive adjectives, the possessive pronouns also change according to the gender and the number of the noun they replace.

|  | Masculine | Feminine | Masc. Plural | Fem. Plural |  |
|---|---|---|---|---|---|
| Yo | el mío | la mía | los míos | las mías | mine |
| Tú | el tuyo | la tuya | los tuyos | las tuyas | yours |
| El | el suyo | la suya | los suyos | las suyas | his |
| Ella | el suyo | la suya | los suyos | las suyas | hers |
| Nosotr@s | el nuestro | la nuestra | los nuestros | las nuestras | ours |
| Vosotr@s | el vuestro | la vuestra | los vuestros | las vuestras | yours |
| Ell@s | el suyo | la suya | los suyos | las suyas | theirs |

Possessive pronouns are always preceded by a definite article. But after the verb "Ser" the article can be omitted. Examples:

I have read my books and yours.
*He leído mis libros y los tuyos.*

This is mine (a book).
*Este es (el) mío.*

This is his (a bike).
*Esta es suya.*

This is hers (a bike).
*Esta es suya.*

These children are ours.
*Estos niños son nuestros.*

These books are mine.
*Estos libros son míos.*

# 19
# DEMONSTRATIVE ADJECTIVES AND PRONOUNS
## *LOS ADJETIVOS y LOS PRONOMBRES DEMOSTRATIVOS*

## DEMONSTRATIVE ADJECTIVES

Demonstrative adjectives are those adjectives whose function is to point at something. While English only has two options — "this" for something close to you, and "that" for something farther — Spanish has three: *this, that,* and *that over there.* The third option implies an even greater distance.

The demonstrative adjectives are:

| SINGULAR | | PLURAL | |
|---|---|---|---|
| Este *(masc.)* | → **This** | Estos *(masc.)* | → **These** |
| Esta *(fem.)* | | Estas *(fem.)* | |
| (near the speaker) | | | |
| Ese *(masc.)* | → **That** | Esos *(masc.)* | → **Those** |
| Esa *(fem.)* | | Esas *(fem.)* | |
| (near the person adressed) | | | |
| Aquel *(masc.)* | → **That...over there** | | |
| | | Aquellos *(m.)* | → **Those over there** |
| Aquella *(fem.)* | | Aquellas *(f.)* | |
| (remote from both) | | | |

The demonstrative adjectives change according to the noun that they qualify and regularly precede the noun. Examples:

| | | |
|---|---|---|
| these books | *estos libros* | plural masculine |
| these chairs | *estas sillas* | plural feminine |
| this notebook | *este cuaderno* | singular masculine |
| this girl | *esta chica* | singular feminine |

*Este, esta, estos* and *estas (this and these)* are used to point towards nouns which are physically close to the speaker as well as to whomsoever he or she is speaking to, usually within an easy reach. Example:

This car &rarr; Este coche

*Ese, esa, esos* and *esas*

*that and those* are used to point towards nouns which are far away from the speaker, but not necessarily from the listeners. Example:

Those horses &rarr; Esos caballos

*Aquel, aquella, aquellos* and *aquellas (that...over there and those... over there)* are used to point towards nouns which are far away from both the speaker and the listeners. Example:

Those mountains over there &rarr; Aquellas montañas.

## DEMONSTRATIVE PRONOUNS

The demonstrative pronouns are the same in form as the demonstrative adjectives, but they usually have the accent mark: **éste, ése, aquél, ésa, aquélla**, etc.

Thus, if you don't know whether something is masculine or feminine, there is a neuter form for each of the above demonstrative pronouns.

*esto*

*eso*

*aquello*

Use these forms only if you're referring to an abstract idea or an unknown object. For example...

What is that? → ¿Qué es eso?

*Examples:*

You have many books but this one is the best.

*Tiene usted muchos libros, pero este es el mejor.*

Amongst all your dresses, I like this one.

*Entre todos tus vestidos, este es el que me gusta.*

Which trousers do you want? These ones are good, but those ones are better.

*¿Qué pantalones queréis? Estos son buenos, pero aquellos son mejores.*

These tables are from Mumbai, and those ones are from Bilbao.

*Estas mesas son de Mumbai, y aquellas de Bilbao.*

# 20
# OBJECT PRONOUNS
## *PRONOMBRES COMPLEMENTO*

### DIRECT OBJECT PRONOUNS

In Spanish, the object pronouns express the object of the verb. In the sentence,

> (yo) Envío una carta. → I sent a letter.

the subject is omitted, *envío* is the verb, and *una carta* is the direct object. In English, we can replace "a letter" with a pronoun:

> I sent it. → "it" is a direct object pronoun.

The same occurs in Spanish. We can replace "una carta" with the object pronoun "**la**", because *carta* is feminine.

> (yo) Envío una carta. → (yo) *La* envío.

Note that in Spanish the direct object pronoun is placed directly before the verb when it is conjugated, or is attached to the end of the infinitive or imperative forms:

| | | |
|---|---|---|
| *Pedro sabe la solución.* | → | *Pedro **la** sabe.* |
| Pedro knows the solution. | → | Pedro knows it. |
| *Envía (tú) la carta.* | → | *Envíala.* |
| Send the letter. | → | Send it. |

Here is a list of subjects with the direct object pronouns:

| | | | |
|---|---|---|---|
| YO | → | **ME** | me |
| TÚ | → | **TE** | you |
| ÉL | → | **LO** | him |
| usted (male) | | | you |
| | | | it |
| ELLA | → | **LA** | her |
| usted (female) | | | you |
| | | | it |
| NOSOTR@S | → | **NOS** | us |
| VOSOTR@S | → | **OS** | you |
| ELLOS | → | **LOS** | them |
| ustedes (male) | | | you |
| ELLAS | → | **LAS** | them |
| ustedes (female) | | | you |

Note that in the third person forms (**LO**, **LA**, **LOS**, **LAS**), the pronouns change their number and gender, depending on the noun they replace. *Examples*:

Tengo un coche.  → **LO** tengo.  masculine singular
I have a car.

Leo una revista.  → **LA** leo.  feminine singular
I read a magazine.

Compro libros.  → **LOS** compro. masculine plural
I buy books.

Como manzanas.  → **LAS** como.  feminine plural
I eat apples.

The direct object can also be a person.

> I know you.
> *Te conozco.*
> She loves me.
> *Ella me ama.*
> Juan sees her.
> *Juan la ve.*
> They call us.
> *Ellos nos llaman.*

## INDIRECT OBJECT PRONOUNS

The indirect object answers the question "To whom?" or "For whom?"

He gives Miguel the book.

To whom does he give the book?   → To Miguel.

He buys me flowers.

For whom does he buy the flowers? → For me.

In Spanish, we would translate the sentence "He gives Miguel the book" as follows:

> *(él) Da el libro a Miguel.*

In the sentence, the subject "**él**" is omitted, *da* is the verb, *el libro* is the direct object, and *Miguel* is the indirect object. In English, we can replace "*Miguel*" with a pronoun:

> He gives him the book → "him" is an indirect
> object pronoun.

The same occurs in Spanish. We can replace "*Miguel*" with the object pronoun "*le*" because *Miguel* is singular.

> *(él) Da el libro a Miguel.* → *(él)* **Le** *da el libro.*

In Spanish, the indirect object pronoun is placed directly before the verb when it is conjugated, or is attached at the end of the infinitive or imperative forms. For example:

| | | |
|---|---|---|
| *Pedro compra un regalo a Ana.* | → | *Pedro LE compra un regalo.* |
| Pedro buys Ana a gift. | → | Pedro buys her a gift. |
| *Di la verdad a Ana.* | → | *Dile la verdad.* |
| Tell Ana the truth. | | Tell her the truth. |

Here you have a list of subjects with the indirect object pronouns:

| | | | |
|---|---|---|---|
| YO | → | **ME** | me |
| TÚ | → | **TE** | you |
| ÉL/ELLA | → | **LE** | him/her/it |
| USTED | | | you |
| NOSOTROS | → | **NOS** | us |
| VOSOTROS | → | **OS** | you |
| ELL@S | → | **LES** | them |
| USTEDES | | | you |

Note that in the third person forms (**LE, LES**), the pronouns change their number depending on the noun they replace. *Examples*:

Yo *le* explico la lección *a Manolo.*

→ Yo *le* explico la lección.

Yo *les* explico la lección *a los estudiantes.*

→ Yo *les* explico la lección.

Spanish prefers to use the indirect object pronouns even when the indirect object is mentioned:

*Le estoy escribiendo una carta **a Gaurang**.*

I am writing a letter to Gaurang.

## DOUBLE PRONOUN

As we have seen, both the object pronouns must come before the conjugated verb. In Spanish, the indirect pronoun always comes first. Let's see an example:

*Te doy el dinero.*        → TE  LO  doy

I give you the money.       *ind.  dir.*

When the indirect pronoun is referred to a third person, we must change LE or LES for **SE**. Example:

*Le doy el dinero.*       → LE  LO  doy *is incorrect.*

I give him the money.    → **SE**  LO  doy *is correct.*

## VERB GUSTAR

There is a group of verbs that are most frequently used with indirect objects. The most common is **gustar**, which is the equivalent of *to like*, but functions very differently. In English, the expression "I like the film" makes *I* the subject and *the film* the object. In *"Me gusta la película"*, *la película* is the subject of the sentence and *me* is the indirect object.

It is as if we were to say in English *"The film is pleasing to me"*: **La película me gusta**. See some examples:

| | |
|---|---|
| We like cricket. | → *Nos gusta el cricket.* |
| Peter likes cooking. | → *A Peter le gusta cocinar.* |
| Do you like the book? | → *¿Te gusta el libro?* |
| Yes, I like it. | → *Sí, me gusta.* |

# 21
# FUTURE TENSE
## *EL FUTURO*

The future tense of regular verbs is formed by directly adding the following endings to the verb in the infinitive form.

| é | ás | á | emos | éis | án |
|---|----|---|------|-----|----|

*Examples*:

## Mirar (to watch)

| (yo) | é | miraré | I will watch |
|------|---|--------|--------------|
| (tú) | ás | mirarás | You will watch |
| (él/ella) | á | mirará | He/She/It will watch |
| (nosotros) | emos | miraremos | We will watch |
| (vosotros) | éis | miraréis | You all will watch |
| (ell@s) | án | mirarán | They will watch |

I will watch the children in the garden.
*Miraré a los niños en el jardín.*

## Ver (to see)

| veré | I will see |
|------|-----------|
| verás | You will see |
| verá | He/She/It will see |
| veremos | We will see |

| veréis | You all will see |
| verán | They will see |

I will see the birds in the sky.
*Veré los pajaros en el cielo.*

**Partir (to leave)**

| partiré | I will leave |
| partirás | You will leave |
| partirá | He/She/It will leave |
| partiremos | We will leave |
| partiréis | You all will leave |
| partirán | They will leave |

She shall leave in a few minutes.
*Partirá en unos minutos.*

However, there are certain exceptions to irregular verbs. The endings remain the same but the stem of the verb changes:

| *caber* | to fit in | *cabré, cabrás...* |
| *decir* | to say | *diré, dirás...* |
| *haber* | to have | *habré, habrás...* |
| *hacer* | to do | *haré, harás...* |
| *poder* | to be able to | *podré, podrás...* |
| *poner* | to put | *pondré, pondrás...* |
| *querer* | to want | *querré, querrás...* |
| *saber* | to know | *sabré, sabrás...* |
| *salir* | to go out/ come out | *suldré, suldrás...* |
| *tener* | to have | *tendré, tendrás...* |
| *valer* | to be worth | *valdré, valdrás...* |
| *venir* | to come | *vendré, vendrás...* |

# NEAR FUTURE

The *futuro próximo* is used to show the near future, that is, when an action is going to take place in a very short period of time. It is used with the verb *ir* (to go) and the preposition "a". The following formula is used:

$$ir + a + verb \text{ (in the infinitive form)}$$

*Example* : I am going to eat.
>*Voy a comer.*

She is going to see a film.
>*Va a ver una película.*

Thus, a sentence in *futuro próximo* can be further translated as 'going to' in English.

The *negative* form of *'futuro próximo'* is formed by adding **NO** before the verb *'ir'*. For example:

I am not going to drink water.
>*No voy a beber agua.*

We are not going to talk to María.
>*No vamos a hablar con María.*

The interrogative form of *'futuro próximo'* is formed by simply adding a question mark at the end of the statement. For example:

You are going to Mexico.
>*Vais a ir a Méjico.*

Are you going to Mexico?
>*¿Vais a ir a Méjico?*

# 22
# CONDITIONAL
## *CONDICIONAL*

The conditional tense is used to indicate that an action or state of being is dependent on the occurrence of a condition. Frequently, the conditional is used to express probability, possibility, wonder or conjecture, and is usually translated as would, could, must have or probably.

The conditional has the same stem as for the future tense. To conjugate -ar, -er and -ir (regular verbs) in the conditional, simply add one of the following to the infinitive:

| ía | ías | ía | íamos | íais | ían |
|----|-----|----|-------|------|-----|

*Examples*:

## HABLAR (to speak)

| (yo) | ía | hablaría | I would speak |
|------|-----|----------|---------------|
| (tú) | ías | hablarías | You would speak |
| (él) | ía | hablaría | He/She would speak |
| (nosotro@) | íamos | hablaríamos | We would speak |
| (vosotr@s) | íais | hablaríais | You would speak |
| (ell@s) | ían | hablarían | They would speak |

## COMER (to eat)

| (yo) | comería | I would eat |
|---|---|---|
| (tú) | comerías | You would eat |
| (él) | comería | He/She would eat |
| (nosotr@s) | comeríamos | We would eat |
| (vosotr@s) | comeríais | You would eat |
| (ell@s) | comerían | They would eat |

## VIVIR (to live)

| (yo) | viviría | I would live |
|---|---|---|
| (tú) | vivirías | You would live |
| (él) | viviría | He/She would live |
| (nosotr@s) | viviríamos | We would live |
| (vosotr@s) | viviríais | You would live |
| (ell@s) | vivirían | They would live |

The same twelve common verbs that are irregular in the future tense are also irregular in the conditional tense. Their endings are regular, but their stems change in the same way as they change in the future tense:

| *caber* | to fit in | *cabría, cabrías...* |
|---|---|---|
| *decir* | to say | *diría, dirías...* |
| *haber* | to have | *habría, habrías...* |
| *hacer* | to do | *haría, harías...* |
| *poder* | to be able to | *podría, podrías...* |
| *poner* | to put | *pondría, pondrías...* |
| *querer* | to want | *querría, querrías...* |
| *saber* | to know | *sabría, sabrías...* |
| *salir* | to go out | *saldría, saldrías...* |
| *tener* | to have | *tendría, tendrías...* |
| *valer* | to be worth | *valdría, valdrías...* |
| *venir* | to come | *vendría, vendrías...* |

**Some examples :**

The student said that he would study for one more hour.

*El alumno dijo que **estudiaría** una hora más.*

We were probably busy when you called.

***Estaríamos** ocupados cuando llamaste.*

It would be interesting to study Chinese.

***Sería** interesante estudiar chino.*

Could you please tell me what time the cinema opens?

*Por favor, ¿**podría** decirme a qué hora abre el cine?*

Which one would you buy?

*¿Cuál **compraría** usted?*

I would prefer to eat at three o'clock.

***Preferiría** comer a las tres.*

We should eat at Cataluna restaurant.

***Deberíamos** cenar en el restaurante Cataluña.*

I would like to live in Chile.

*Me **gustaría** vivir en Chile.*

# 23
# PRESENT PERFECT TENSE
## *PRETÉRITO PERFECTO COMPUESTO*

The present perfect tense in Spanish is formed with the present tense of the auxiliary verb *haber* and the past participles of the verb.

We have already seen the conjugation of the auxiliary verb *haber*:

> he
>
> has
>
> ha
>
> hemos
>
> habéis
>
> han

The past participles are formed by adding **ado** to –*ar* ending verbs and **ido** to -*er* and –*ir* ending verbs.

| | |
|---|---|
| mirar | mir**ado** (watched) |
| comer | com**ido** (eaten) |
| partir | part**ido** (left) |

*Examples*:

> I have eaten.
>
> *He comido.*

He has sold the house.

*Ha vendido la casa.*

They have learnt the lesson.

*Han aprendido la lección.*

Accents are put on the past participles of a few verbs. Examples:

| | | |
|---|---|---|
| *caer* | *caído* | (fallen) |
| *leer* | *leído* | (read) |
| *creer* | *creído* | (believed) |
| *oír* | *oído* | (heard) |

Given below is a list of past participles of a few commonly used verbs. Note that there are also a few irregular past participles:

| Verb | Past participle | |
|---|---|---|
| *ser* | *sido* | been |
| *estar* | *estado* | been |
| *haber* | *habido* | had |
| *tener* | *tenido* | had |
| *hacer* | *hecho* | done |
| *venir* | *venido* | come |
| *ir* | *ido* | gone |
| *salir* | *salido* | left |
| *nacer* | *nacido* | born |
| *morir* | *muerto* | died |
| *abrir* | *abierto* | opened |
| *cubrir* | *cubierto* | covered |
| *beber* | *bebido* | drunk |

| | | |
|---|---|---|
| *ver* | *visto* | seen |
| *leer* | *leído* | read |
| *decir* | *dicho* | said |
| *recibir* | *recibido* | received |
| *poner* | *puesto* | put |
| *coger* | *cogido* | taken |
| *aprender* | *aprendido* | learnt |
| *comprender* | *comprendido* | understood |
| *sentarse* | *sentado* | sat |
| *esperar* | *esperado* | waited |
| *golpear* | *golpeado* | beaten |
| *elegir* | *elegido* | chosen |
| *conducir* | *conducido* | driven |
| *conocer* | *conocido* | known |
| *bajar* | *bajado* | descended |
| *oír* | *oído* | heard |
| *correr* | *corrido* | run |
| *creer* | *creído* | believed |
| *descubrir* | *descubierto* | discovered |
| *llegar a ser* | *llegado a ser* | become |
| *dormir* | *dormido* | slept |
| *escribir* | *escrito* | written |
| *deber* | *debido* | must |
| *ofrecer* | *ofrecido* | offered |
| *pintar* | *pintado* | painted |
| *poder* | *podido* | could |
| *querer* | *querido* | wanted |
| *llover* | *llovido* | rained |

| | | |
|---|---|---|
| *perder* | *perdido* | lost |
| *permitir* | *permitido* | allowed |
| *producir* | *producido* | produced |
| *reconocer* | *reconocido* | recognised |
| *devolver* | *devuelto* | returned |
| *responder* | *respondido* | answered |
| *reír* | *reído* | laughed |
| *saber* | *sabido* | known |
| *sentir* | *sentido* | felt/smelt |
| *seguir* | *seguido* | followed |
| *vender* | *vendido* | sold |
| *vivir* | *vivido* | lived |

For 'ar' ending verbs, we add 'ado' in the past participle and for 'ir'/'er' verbs, we add 'ido' in the past participle.

# 24
# SIMPLE PAST
## PRETÉRITO PERFECTO SIMPLE

Spanish has two simple past tenses, known as the preterite and the imperfect indicative. The simple past in English such as "he drank" can be translated in Spanish using either the preterite (*bebió*) or the imperfect indicative (*bebía*), but the two tenses are not interchangeable. In general, the preterite is used when expressing an action which took place at a definite time in the past. Whereas, the imperfect tense, as the name suggests is used to refer to an action that doesn't have a specific ending.

The actions that have a definite beginning and a definite end are expressed by the simple past tense. When conjugating regular verbs in the simple past form, you must drop the endings "**ar**", "**er**" or "**ir**" and add the endings according to the subject.

To conjugate regular **-ar** verbs in the preterite, replace the ending (**-ar**) with the following:

| é | aste | ó | amos | asteis | aron |
|---|------|---|------|--------|------|

**HABLAR (to speak)**

| (yo) | -é | hablé | I spoke... |
|------|------|-----------|------------|
| (tú) | -aste | hablaste | |
| (él) | -ó | habló | |

| (nosotr@s) | **-amos** | hablamos |
| (vosotr@s) | **–asteis** | hablasteis |
| (ell@s) | **–aron** | hablaron |

To conjugate regular **-er** and **-ir** verbs in the preterite, replace the ending with the following:

| í | iste | ió | imos | isteis | ieron |

## COMER

| (yo) com**í** | I ate... |
| (tú) com**iste** | |
| (él) com**ió** | |
| (nosotros) com**imos** | |
| (vosotros) com**isteis** | |
| (ell@s) com**ieron** | |

## ABRIR

| (yo) abr**í** | I opened... |
| (tú) abr**iste** | |
| (él) abr**ió** | |
| (nosotros) abr**imos** | |
| (vosotros) abr**isteis** | |
| (ell@s) abr**ieron** | |

The preterite is used:

- to tell something that happened once

  They arrived at eight o'clock.

  *Ellos llegaron a las ocho.*

- for actions that were repeated a specific number of times, or occurred during a specific period of time

  We lived there for four years.

  *Vivimos allí durante cuatro años.*

- to state the beginning or the end of an action

  The hurricane started at 8.

  *El huracán comenzó a las ocho.*

## IRREGULAR VERBS

When conjugating the preterite, some irregular verbs must be considered. The endings remain the same but the stem of the verb changes:

| | | |
|---|---|---|
| *caber* | to fit in | *cupe, cupiste...* |
| *decir* | to say | *dije, dijiste...* |
| *haber* | to have | *hube, hubiste...* |
| *hacer* | to do | *hice, hiciste...* |
| *poder* | to be able to | *pude, pudiste...* |
| *poner* | to put | *puse, pusiste...* |
| *querer* | to want | *quise, quisiste...* |
| *saber* | to know | *supe, supiste...* |
| *salir* | to go out | *salí, saliste...* |
| *tener* | to have | *tuve, tuviste...* |
| *ir* | to go | *fui, fuiste* |
| *ser* | to be | *fui, fuiste* |
| *estar* | to be | *estuve, estuviste* |
| *venir* | to come | *vine, viniste...* |

Notice that "*ser*" (to be) and "*ir*" (to go) present the same conjugation in the preterite tense. *Example*:

**Fui** *a Manila durante aquellas vacaciones.*

I went to Manila during those holidays.

**Fui** *muy feliz durante aquellas vacaciones.*

I was very happy during those holidays.

# 25
# SIMPLE PAST — IMPERFECT
## PRETÉRITO IMPERFECTO

In general, the imperfect is the tense that expresses an incomplete action in the past, that occurred repeatedly or frequently, or that took place over an indefinite period of time. It is used to refer to an action that doesn't have a specific ending. We "set scenes" using the imperfect tense.

As we saw with the preterite tense, when conjugating regular verbs in the imperfect form, you must preserve the root of the verb and replace the endings "ar", "er" or "ir".

To conjugate regular "-ar" verbs in the preterite, simply drop the ending (-ar) and add one of the following:

**aba      abas      aba      ábamos      abais      aban**

## HABLAR

| (yo)      | -aba     | hablaba    | I was speaking... |
|-----------|----------|------------|-------------------|
| (tú)      | -abas    | hablabas   |                   |
| (él)      | -aba     | hablaba    |                   |
| (nosotr@s) | –ábamos | hablábamos |                   |
| (vosotr@s) | –abais  | hablabais  |                   |
| (ell@s)   | –aban    | hablaban   |                   |

To conjugate regular "-er" and "-ir" verbs in the preterite, simply drop the ending and add one of the following:

| ía | ías | ía | íamos | íais | ían |
|----|-----|-----|-------|------|-----|

**COMER**

(yo) com**ía**  I was eating...
(tú) com**ías**
(él) com**ía**
(nosotr@s) com**íamos**
(vosotr@s) com**íais**
(ell@s) com**ían**

**ABRIR**

(yo) abr**ía**  I was opening...
(tú) abr**ías**
(él) abr**ía**
(nosotr@s) abr**íamos**
(vosotr@s) abr**íais**
(ell@s) abr**ían**

The imperfect is used:

- to describe in the past: the background or setting, situations, conditions and actions that were in progress:

    It was six o'clock. Pedro was ill and it was raining outside.
    **Eran** las seis. Pedro **estaba** enfermo y **llovía** afuera.

- to describe habitual actions that used to take place in the past without specific reference to a beginning or end:

    They used to go to the cinema every Sunday.
    **Iban** al cine todos los domingos.

    Javier was rich because he worked a lot.
    Javier **era** rico porque **trabajaba** mucho.

- for actions that set the "stage" for another action:

    I was laughing when my father entered.
    Yo **reía** cuando entró mi padre.

# IRREGULAR VERBS

There are only three verbs that are irregular in the imperfect tense: *ser, ir* and *ver*. Let's see how they are conjugated:

|           | IR (to go) | SER (to be) | VER (to see) |
|-----------|------------|-------------|--------------|
| (yo)      | iba        | era         | veía         |
| (tú)      | ibas       | eras        | veías        |
| (él/ella) | iba        | era         | veía         |
| (nosotr@s)| íbamos     | éramos      | veíamos      |
| (vosotr@s)| ibais      | erais       | veíais       |
| (ell@s)   | iban       | eran        | veían        |

# 26
# SUBJUNCTIVE MOOD — PRESENT
## PRESENTE DEL SUBJUNTIVO

So far, we have seen verb forms which are used to make straightforward statements or to ask questions. In almost all grammatically simple sentences, the verb is in the indicative mood:

*Esto es muy complicado.*
This is very complicated.

*Las niñas jugaban en el parque.*
The girls played in the park.

*¿Vas a Cáceres este invierno?*
Are you going to Caceres this winter?

The **subjunctive mood** is used to show actions which are: impossible, possible or probable, hypothetical, desired, requested, due to take place in the future. Spanish speakers use the subjunctive regularly. The subjunctive mood is used to express everything except certainty and objectivity: things like doubt, uncertainty, or subjectivity. Examples:

I doubt that it is cold in Spain.
*Dudo de que en España haga frío.*

I hope that Amay uses his bicycle.
*Espero que Amay utilice su bici.*

In order to form the present subjunctive, use the first person singular of the present indicative and remove the ending. To conjugate regular -ar verbs, simply add the following endings:

| e | es | e | emos | éis | en |
|---|----|----|------|-----|-----|

## HABLAR

(yo) hable                ...that I speak...
(tú) hables
(él) hable
(nosotr@s) hablemos
(vosotr@s) habléis
(ell@s) hablen

To conjugate regular -er and -ir verbs, simply add the following endings:

| a | as | a | amos | áis | an |
|---|----|----|------|-----|-----|

## COMER                ABRIR

(yo) coma   ...that I eat...   (yo) abra  ...that I open...
(tú) comas                   (tú) abras
(él) coma                     (él) abra
(nosotr@s) comamos       (nosotr@s) abramos
(vosotr@s) comáis          (vosotr@s) abráis
(ell@s) coman             (ell@s) abran

Note that the irregular endings and spelling changes in the first person singular of the present indicative, appear in all persons of the present subjunctive.

**Example:**

|  | Present indicative | Present subjunctive |
|---|---|---|
| verb PEDIR (to ask) → | (yo) pid**o** → | (yo) pid**a** |
| verb TENER (to have) | (yo) teng**o** | (yo) teng**a** |

However, the following six verbs do not follow the rules explained above to form the present subjunctive because their present indicative doesn't end in **o**:

|  | Present Indicative | Present subjunctive |  |
|---|---|---|---|
| estar → | (yo) estoy | (yo) esté, (tú) estés... | that I am... |
| dar → | (yo) doy | (yo) dé, (tú) des... | that I give... |
| haber → | (yo) he | (yo) haya, (tú) hayas... | that I have... |
| ir → | (yo) voy | (yo) vaya, (tú) vayas... | that I go... |
| saber → | (yo) sé | (yo) sepa, (tú) sepas... | that I know... |
| ser | (yo) soy | (yo) sea, (tú) seas... | that I am... |

## USES

The subjunctive mood is used when:

- the main verb expresses negation, doubt or desire:

    I don't think that she is in Madrid.
    *No creo que ella esté en Madrid.*

- the main clause says that the subordinate one is impossible, probable, incredible or doubtful, also necessary or desired;

    It's impossible that it is true!
    *¡Es imposible que sea cierto!*

    I hope you are happy in Venezuela.
    *Espero que seas feliz en Venezuela.*

- someone wants, requires, asks, needs, allows or orders someone to do something:

> I want you to come to Los Angeles.
> *Quiero que vengas a Los Ángeles.*

Don't forget that subjunctive is used to talk about uncertainty. The indicative mood talks mostly of certitude. Compare the next two lists:

| Expression + indicative | | Expression + subjunctive |
|---|---|---|
| *afirmar que...* | to affirm/to deny | *negar que...* |
| *creer que...* | to believe/not | *no creer que...* |
| *está claro que...* | it's clear/not | *no está claro que...* |
| *está convencido de que...* | it's convinced/not | *no está convencido de que...* |
| *está seguro de que...* | it's sure/not | *no está seguro de que...* |
| *es verdad que...* | it's true/not | *no es verdad que...* |
| *imaginar que...* | to imagine/not | *no imaginarse que...* |
| *es cierto que...* | it's certain/doubtful | *es dudoso que ...* |

# 27
# IMPERATIVE
## *EL IMPERATIVO*

The Imperative Mood is the form used to give an order, to give advice or to beg for something. It only has one tense, that is, the present tense. We use different command forms when giving an order as we address people both formally and informally. Example:

Buy the books.

*Compra los libros* (you, singular informal) → (tú)
*Compre los libros* (you, singular formal) → (usted)
*Comprad los libros* (you, plural informal) → (vosotros)
*Compren los libros* (you, plural formal) → (ustedes)

It is important to note that the command statements in the *nosotros* form is never used. When conjugating regular verbs in the simple imperative, you must replace the endings "**ar**", "**er**" or "**ir**", as we have seen in the earlier lessons. Note that the Spanish imperative exists for five different subjects: "*tú*", "*usted*", "*nosotr@s*", "*vosotr@s*", and "*ustedes*". Note that the formal commands "usted" and "ustedes", and "nosotros" are formed in the same way as the **present subjunctive** (*see lesson 26*) and take the special cases as well.

To conjugate regular "**-ar**" verbs in the imperative mood, simply drop the ending -ar and add one of the following:

Example: **HABLAR**

| (tú) | **a** | Hab**la** | **Speak!** |
|---|---|---|---|
| (usted) | **e** | Habl**e** | |
| (nosotr@s) | **emos** | Habl**emos** | |
| (vosotr@s) | **ad** | Habl**ad** | |
| (ustedes) | **en** | Habl**en** | |

To conjugate regular **-er** verbs in the imperative mood, simply drop the ending and add one of the following:

Example: **COMER**

| (tú) | **e** | Com**e** | **Eat!** |
|---|---|---|---|
| (usted) | **a** | Com**a** | |
| (nosotr@s) | **amos** | Com**amos** | |
| (vosotr@s) | **ed** | Com**ed** | |
| (ustedes) | **an** | Com**an** | |

To conjugate regular **-ir** verbs in the imperative mood, simply drop the ending and add one of the following:

Example: **ABRIR**

| (tú) | **e** | Abr**e** | **Open!** |
|---|---|---|---|
| (usted) | **a** | Abr**a** | |
| (nosotr@s) | **amos** | Abr**amos** | |
| (vosotr@s) | **id** | Abr**id** | |
| (ustedes) | **an** | Abr**an** | |

The imperative is used only affirmatively. To form the negative commands in Spanish, the present subjunctive is used. For example:

(tú)        Speak! → Habla   → Don't speak! → No hables
(usted)     Speak! → Hable   → Don't speak! → No hable
(vosotr@s) Speak! → Hablad → Don't speak! → No habléis
(ustedes)  Speak! → Hablen → Don't speak! → No hablen

## USES

We use the imperative mood to give orders or commands to a second person. Example:

> Open the door, please.
> *Abre (tú) la puerta, por favor.*

As we can see from the above example, in the affirmative form of the imperative mood, the subject of the verb goes after the verb, but they are usually omitted.

When we want to give an order or command with a negative sentence, we do not use the imperative mood but the present simple tense of the subjunctive mood. Example:

> Do not get home late tonight.
> *No vengas (tú) tarde esta noche.*

For prohibitions, we will once again use the present tense of the subjunctive mood. Example:

> Do not smoke here.
> *No fumes aquí.*

# 28
# COUNTRIES AND NATIONALITIES
## *LOS PAÍSES y LAS NACIONALIDADES*

In Spanish, we put articles before the names of a few countries but most of the countries are named without articles. There is no rule which would help you decide which one would carry an article and which one wouldn't. You either need to memorize or to pick up as you learn the names of the countries and hear them being used. Following is a list of countries as named in Spanish:

**COUNTRIES**
*Los paises*

| | |
|---|---|
| India | *la India* |
| Spain | *España* |
| France | *Francia* |
| Japan | *Japón* |
| China | *China* |
| Switzerland | *Suiza* |
| England | *Inglaterra* |
| Portugal | *Portugal* |
| Mexico | *Méjico* |
| Hungary | *Hungría* |
| Pakistan | *Paquistán* |
| United States (of America) | *los Estados Unidos (de América)* |

| | |
|---|---|
| Morocco | *Marruecos* |
| Belgium | *Bélgica* |
| Italy | *Italia* |
| Germany | *Alemania* |
| Russia | *Rusia* |
| Canada | *Canadá* |
| Zimbabwe | *Zimbabue* |
| Sri Lanka | *Sri Lanka* |
| Holland | *Holanda* |
| Egypt | *Egipto* |
| Brazil | *Brasil* |
| Congo | *Congo* |
| Gabon | *Gabón* |
| Algeria | *Argelia* |
| Tunisia | *Túnez* |
| Vietnam | *Vietnam* |
| Senegal | *Senegal* |
| Nigeria | *Nigeria* |
| Mauritania | *Mauritania* |
| Madagascar | *Madagascar* |
| Cambodia | *Camboya* |
| Burkina Faso | *Burkina Faso* |
| Luxembourg | *Luxemburgo* |
| Australia | *Australia* |
| Scotland | *Escocia* |
| Wales | *el País de Gales* |
| Ireland | *Irlanda* |
| Zambia | *Zambia* |
| Austria | *Austria* |
| Mauritius | *Isla Mauricio* |
| Myanmar | *Myanmar* |

# NATIONALITIES
## Las nacionalidades

The nationalities in Spanish vary according to the number and gender. "–o" is changed to "–a" in the nationalities ending with "-o". Nationalities ending with "-és" are changed to feminine by changing the ending to "-esa". Nationalities with other endings don't have separate masculine and feminine forms. Although many other adjectives of nationality end with a consonant, these adjectives **do not** follow the same rules as other adjectives ending in a consonant, rather, they have a distinct feminine form ending with "-a".

a French boy
*un chico francés*

a French girl
*una chica francesa*

an Indian boy
*un chico indio*

an Indian girl
*una chica india*

We generally add "-s" to change it to plural. For example,

an Indian boy
*un chico indio*

Indian boys
*Unos chicos indios*

| Nationality | Masculine Form | Feminine Form |
| --- | --- | --- |
| Indian | *indio* | *india* |
| Spaniard | *español* | *española* |
| Argentine | *argentino* | *argentina* |
| Chilean | *chileno* | *chilena* |
| Paraguayan | *paraguayo* | *paraguaya* |
| Uruguayan | *uruguayo* | *uruguaya* |
| Bolivian | *boliviano* | *boliviana* |
| Ecuadorian | *ecuatoriano* | *ecuatoriana* |
| Peruvian | *peruano* | *peruana* |
| Venezuelan | *venezolano* | *venezolana* |
| Colombian | *colombiano* | *colombiana* |
| Guatemalan | *guatemalteco* | *guatemalteca* |
| Costa Rican | *costarricense* | *costarricense* |
| Honduran | *hondureño* | *hondureña* |
| Nicaraguan | *nicaragüense* | *nicaragüense* |
| Salvadoran | *salvadoreño* | *salvadoreña* |
| Dominican | *dominicano* | *dominicana* |
| Cuban | *cubano* | *cubana* |
| Mexican | *mejicano* | *mejicana* |
| French | *francés* | *francesa* |
| Japanese | *japonés* | *japonesa* |
| Chinese | *chino* | *china* |
| American | *americano* | *americana* |
| Swiss | *suizo* | *suiza* |
| English | *inglés* | *inglesa* |
| Portuguese | *portugués* | *portuguesa* |
| Hungarian | *húngaro* | *húngara* |

| | | |
|---|---|---|
| Pakistani | *paquistaní* | *paquistaní* |
| Moroccan | *marroquí* | *marroquí* |
| Belgian | *belga* | *belga* |
| Italian | *italiano* | *italiana* |
| German | *alemán* | *alemana* |
| Russian | *ruso* | *rusa* |
| Canadian | *canadiense* | *canadiense* |
| Sri Lankan | *nativo de Sri Lanka* | *nativa de Sri Lanka* |
| Egyptian | *egipcio* | *egipcia* |
| Brazilian | *brasileño* | *brasileña* |
| Algerian | *argelino* | *argelina* |
| Tunisian | *tunecino* | *tunecina* |
| Senegalese | *senegalés* | *senegalesa* |
| Nigerian | *nigeriano* | *nigeriana* |
| Australian | *australiano* | *australiana* |
| Irish | *irlandés* | *irlandesa* |
| Zimbabwean | *zimbabuo* | *zimbabua* |
| Austrian | *austríaco* | *austríaca* |
| Congolese | *congoleño* | *congoleña* |
| Mauritanian | *mauritano* | *mauritana* |
| Cambodian | *camboyano* | *camboyana* |
| Burmese | *birmano* | *birmana* |
| Scotsman/ woman | *escocés* | *escocesa* |

# 29
# SEASONS
## *LAS ESTACIONES*

### VOCABULARY

| | |
|---|---|
| The season | *la estación* |
| Summer | *el verano* |
| Autumn | *el otoño* |
| Winter | *el invierno* |
| Spring | *la primavera* |
| in summers | *en verano* |
| in autumn | *en otoño* |
| in winters | *en invierno* |
| in spring | *en primavera* |

To describe the weather, we use the verb *"hacer"* (which means 'to do') in the third person singular form, instead of the verb *"ser"* (which means 'to be').

### EXPRESSIONS

How is the weather?
*¿Qué tiempo hace?*

It rains / It is raining.
*Llueve / Está lloviendo.*

It is sunny.
*Hace sol.*

The sun is shining.
*Brilla el sol.*

It snows / It is snowing.
*Nieva / Está nevando.*

The snow falls / The snow is falling.
*La nieve cae.*

It is windy.
*Hace viento.*

It is hot.
*Hace calor.*

It is cold.
*Hace frío.*

It is pleasant.
*Hace bueno.*

It is a bad weather.
*Hace mal tiempo.*

It is foggy.
*Hay niebla.*

# 30
# DIRECTIONS
## *LAS DIRECCIONES*

## COMPASS DIRECTIONS
*Puntos cardinales*

| | |
|---|---|
| North | *el norte* |
| South | *el sur* |
| East | *el este* |
| West | *el oeste* |

## VOCABULARY

| | |
|---|---|
| left | *izquierda* |
| right | *derecha* |
| straight | *recto* |
| straight ahead | *justo enfrente* |
| along | *a lo largo de* |
| turn | *vuelta* |
| in the direction of | *en dirección a* |
| the church | *la iglesia* |
| the shop | *la tienda* |
| the market | *el mercado* |
| the house | *la casa* |
| the cinema | *el cine* |
| the theatre | *el teatro* |
| the hotel | *el hotel* |

| | |
|---|---|
| the school | *la escuela* |
| the airport | *el aeropuerto* |
| the station | *la estación* |
| the bank | *el banco* |
| the bakery | *la panadería* |
| the office | *la oficina* |
| the hospital | *el hospital* |
| the park | *el parque* |
| the garden | *el jardín* |
| the swimming pool | *la piscina* |
| the cafe | *el café* |
| the museum | *el museo* |
| the opera | *la ópera* |
| the disco | *la discoteca* |
| the post office | *Correos* |
| the cathedral | *la catedral* |
| the supermarket | *el supermercado* |
| the beach | *la playa* |
| the restaurant | *el restaurante* |
| the farm | *la granja* |
| the campsite | *el camping / la acampada* |
| the tower | *la torre* |
| the square | *la plaza* |

*Examples*:

How do I reach the bank?
*¿Cómo puedo llegar al banco?* (*llegar*: to reach)

Go straight and then take the first street on the left.
*Siga recto y tome la primese calle a la izquierda.*

How do I go to the hotel?
*¿Cómo puedo llegar al hotel?*

**( 113 )**

Drive along this street.
*Vaya recto a lo largo de esta calle.*

## DIALOGUE

A     *Disculpe, por favor.*
       Excuse me, please.

B     *¿Sí?*
       Yes?

A     *¿Para ir al Hotel Castilla?*
       How do I go to the Castilla Hotel?

B     *Vaya todo recto.*
       Go straight ahead.

       *Tome la segunda calle a la derecha.*
       Then take the second street on the right.

       *Es la calle del Sol.*
       That is del Sol Street.

A     *¿La segunda a la derecha?*
       The second on the right?

B     *Sí, justamente.*
       Yes, exactly.

       *Entonces tome la primera calle a la derecha.*
       Then take the first street on the right.

       *El Hotel Castilla está en la parte izquierda.*
       The Castilla Hotel is on the left.

A     *Muchas gracias. ¡Adiós!*
       Thank you very much. Good bye!

# 31
# FACE AND BODY
## LA CARA y EL CUERPO

## THE FACE
*La cara*

### VOCABULARY

| | |
|---|---|
| the eye | *el ojo* |
| eyes | *los ojos* |
| the nose | *la nariz* |
| the lip | *el labio* |
| the chin | *la barbilla* |
| the cheek | *la mejilla* |
| the ear | *la oreja* |
| the eyelash | *la pestaña* |
| the hair | *el pelo* |
| the moustache | *el bigote* |
| the beard | *la barba* |
| the tooth | *el diente* |
| the tongue | *la lengua* |
| the head | *la cabeza* |
| the mouth | *la boca* |
| the forehead | *la frente* |
| the skull | *el cráneo* |
| the brain | *el cerebro* |

| the eyeball | el globo ocular |
| the eyelid | el párpado |
| the gum | la encía |
| the jaw | la mandíbula |
| the throat | la garganta |

# THE BODY
## El cuerpo

## VOCABULARY

| the limb | el miembro |
| the arm | el brazo |
| the hand | la mano |
| the finger | el dedo |
| the nail | la uña |
| the leg | la pierna |
| the foot | el pie |
| the neck | el cuello |
| the shoulder | el hombro |
| the elbow | el codo |
| the knee | la rodilla |
| the back | la espalda |
| the stomach | el estómago |
| the chest | el pecho |
| the collarbone | la clavícula |
| the lung | el pulmón |
| the heart | el corazón |
| the blood | la sangre |
| the artery | la arteria |
| the muscle | el músculo |
| the windpipe | la tráquea |

| | |
|---|---|
| the thigh | *el muslo* |
| the breast | *el pecho* |
| the rib | *la costilla* |
| the spine | *la columna vertebral* |
| the waist | *la cintura* |
| the abdomen | *el abdomen* |
| the intestine | *el intestino* |
| the kidney | *el riñón* |
| the liver | *el hígado* |
| the uterus | *el útero* |
| the gall bladder | *la vesícula biliar* |
| the urinary bladder | *la vejiga urinaria* |
| the nerve | *el nervio* |
| the forearm | *el antebrazo* |
| the navel | *el ombligo* |
| the thumb | *el pulgar* |
| the index finger | *el dedo índice* |
| the middle finger | *el dedo corazón* |
| the ring finger | *el dedo anular* |
| the little finger | *el dedo meñique* |
| the wrist | *la muñeca* |
| the buttocks | *las nalgas* |
| the pelvis | *la pelvis* |
| the hip | *la cadera* |
| the thigh bone | *el fémur* |
| the kneecap | *la rótula,* |
| the calf | *la pantorrilla* |
| the ankle | *el tobillo* |
| the sole of the foot | *la planta del pie* |
| the toe | *el dedo del pie* |
| the heel | *el talón* |

# 32
# SPORTS AND MUSICAL INSTRUMENTS
## *LOS DEPORTES y LOS INSTRUMENTOS MUSICALES*

## SPORTS
*Los deportes*

### VOCABULARY

| | |
|---|---|
| Hockey | *el hockey* |
| Cricket | *el críquet* |
| Football | *el fútbol* |
| Basketball | *el baloncesto* |
| Volleyball | *el voleibol* |
| Tennis | *el tenis* |
| Table Tennis | *el ping pong* |
| Badminton | *el bádminton* |
| Baseball | *el béisbol* |
| Handball | *el balonmano* |
| Swimming | *la natación* |
| Backstroke | *espalda* |
| Butterfly stroke | *mariposa* |
| Freestyle | *estilo libre* |
| Breast stroke | *braza* |
| Gymnastics | *la gimnasia* |
| Relay | *la carrera de relevos* |

| | |
|---|---|
| Marathon | *la maratón* |
| Sprint | *el sprint* |
| Hurdles | *las vallas* |
| Track and field | *el atletismo* |
| Martial arts | *las artes marciales* |
| Water skiing | *el esquí acuático* |
| Skiing | *el esquí* |
| Alpine skiing | *el esquí alpino* |
| Ice skating | *el patinaje sobre hielo* |
| Roller skating | *el patinaje sobre ruedas* |
| Rugby | *el rugby* |
| Skating | *el patinaje* |
| Skateboard | *el monopatín* |
| Discus | *el disco* |
| Javelin Throw | *el lanzamiento de jabalina* |
| Shot-put | *el lanzamiento de peso* |
| High Jump | *el salto de altura* |
| Long Jump | *el salto de longitud* |
| Fencing | *la esgrima* |
| Wrestling | *la lucha* |
| Water Polo | *el waterpolo* |
| Polo | *el polo* |
| Golf | *el golf* |
| Windsurfing | *el windsurf* |
| Grandstand | *la tribuna* |
| Court | *la pista* |
| Stadium | *el estadio* |
| Snooker | *el billar inglés* |
| Billiards | *el billar* |
| Indoor games | *los deportes en sala* |

| | |
|---|---|
| Match | *el partido* |
| Team | *el equipo* |
| Referee | *el árbitro* |
| Score | *el marcador* |
| Olympics | *los Joegos Olímpicos* |
| Asian Games | *los Juegos de Asia* |
| Championship | *el campeonato* |
| League | *la Liga* |
| Quarter-finals | *los cuartos de final* |
| Semi-final | *los semifinales* |
| Final | *la final* |
| Runner up | *el subcampeón* |
| To win | *ganar* |
| To lose | *perder* |
| To participate | *participar* |
| Athletics | *el atletismo* |
| Cycling | *el ciclismo* |
| Horse-riding | *la equitación* |
| Sailing | *la vela* |
| Fishing | *la pesca* |
| Game | *el juego* |
| Chess | *el ajedrez* |
| Hiking | *el senderismo* |
| Hunting | *la caza* |
| Jogging | *el jogging* |
| Archery | *el tiro con arco* |
| Boxing | *el boxeo* |
| Diving | *el submarinismo* |
| Board games | *los juegos de mesa* |
| Computer games | *los videojuegos* |

# MUSICAL INSTRUMENTS
## Los instrumentos musicales

### VOCABULARY

| | |
|---|---|
| Violin | *el violín* |
| Guitar | *la guitarra* |
| Piano | *el piano* |
| Flute | *la flauta* |
| Xylophone | *el xilófono* |
| Mouth organ | *la armónica* |
| Bagpipes | *la gaita* |
| Harmonium | *el armonio* |
| Clarinet | *el clarinete* |
| Bugle | *el clarín* |
| Drum | *el tambor* |
| Bell | *la campana* |
| Accordion | *el acordeón* |
| Saxophone | *el saxofón* |
| Harp | *el arpa* |
| Trumpet | *la trompeta* |
| Celtic / Irish harp | *el arpa irlandesa* |

## DIALOGUE

Tanya : Are you a sportsman (sportswoman)?
*¿Eres deportista?*

Juan : Yes I am a sportsman.
*Sí, soy deportista.*

Tanya : Do you like sports?
*¿Te gusta el deporte?*

Juan : Yes, I love sports.
*Sí, me encanta el deporte.*

Tanya : What sport do you play?
*¿Qué deportes practicas?*

Juan : I play tennis and I swim.
*Juego al tenis y practico natación.*

Tanya : Do you play a musical instrument?
*¿Toca usted algún instrumento musical?*

Juan : No, I don't play any instrument.
*No, no sé tocar ningún instrumento.*

With instruments, the verb 'tocar' is used.

I play piano.
*Toco el piano.*

I play violin.
*Toco el violín.*

I play guitar.
*Toco la guitarra.*

I play accordion.
*Toco el acordeón.*

I play drums.
*Toco la batería.*

With sports, the verbs "practicar" and 'jugar' are used.

I play cricket.
*Juego al cricket*

I play chess.
*Juego al ajedrez.*

# 33
# MEALS
## *LAS COMIDAS*

## VOCABULARY

| | |
|---|---|
| Breakfast | *el desayuno* |
| Lunch | *la comida* |
| Snacks | *la merienda* |
| Dinner | *la cena* |
| To drink | *beber* |
| To eat | *comer* |
| To take | *tomar* |
| Starters | *Entremeses* |
| | *Aperitivo* |
| | *Entrada* |
| | *Primer plato* |
| main course | *Segundo plato* |
| | *Plato principal* |
| sweet/dessert | *el postre* |
| Menu | *Menú* |

*Examples*:

I have my breakfast.

*Estoy tomando el desayuno. / Estoy desayunando.*

I have my lunch.

*Estoy tomando la comida. / Estoy comiendo.*

I have my snacks.

*Estoy tomando la merienda. / Estoy merendando.*

I have my dinner.

*Estoy tomando la cena. / Estoy cenando.*

## QUANTITY

| | |
|---|---|
| a box of | *una caja de* |
| a tin of | *un bote de* |
| a bottle of | *una botella de* |
| a litre of | *un litro de* |
| a piece of | *un trozo de* |
| a packet of | *un paquete de* |
| a portion of | *una porción de* |
| a slice of | *una loncha de* |
| a kilo of | *un kilo de* |
| half a kilo of | *medio kilo de* |
| 10 grams of | *diez gramos de* |

## SHOPS
*Tiendas*

| | |
|---|---|
| butcher's | *la carnicería* |
| baker's | *la panadería* |
| grocer's | *el ultramarinos* |
| cake shop | *la pastelería* |
| pork butcher's | *la charcutería* |
| tobacconist's | *el estanco* |
| dairy | *la lechería* |
| fish store | *la pescadería* |

# THINGS TO EAT
## Cosas para comer

| | |
|---|---|
| butter | *la mantequilla* |
| biscuit | *la galleta* |
| carrot | *la zanahoria* |
| jam | *la mermelada* |
| croissant | *el cruasán* |
| potato chips | *las patatas fritas* |
| cheese | *el queso* |
| honey | *la miel* |
| bread | *el pan* |
| peas | *los guisantes* |
| pizza | *la pizza* |
| fish | *el pescado* |
| soup | *la sopa* |
| salad | *la ensalada* |
| fruit salad | *la ensalada de frutas* |
| vegetables | *las verduras* |
| lettuce | *la lechuga* |
| cauliflower | *la coliflor* |
| green beans | *las judías verdes* |
| potato | *la patata* |
| sweets | *los caramelos* |
| the ice cream | *el helado* |
| the hot dog | *el perrito caliente* |
| ham | *el jamón* |
| onion | *la cebolla* |
| pork | *el cerdo* |
| chicken | *el pollo* |

| | |
|---|---|
| fillet | *el filete* |
| beef | *la carne de vaca, la carne de res* |
| steak | *el bistec* |
| lollipop | *chupachup* |
| sandwich | *el bocadillo* |
| tomato | *el tomate* |
| mushroom | *el champiñón* |
| flour | *la harina* |
| lamb | *el cordero* |
| mustard | *la mostaza* |
| rabbit | *el conejo* |
| veal | *la ternera* |
| omelette | *la tortilla* |
| yoghurt | *el yogur* |
| salt | *la sal* |
| pepper | *la pimienta* |
| oil | *el aceite* |
| vinegar | *el vinagre* |
| cake | *el pastel* |
| tart | *la tarta* |
| pancake | *la tortita* |
| sausage | *la salchicha* |
| chocolate mousse | *la mousse de chocolate* |
| caramel cream | *el flan* |
| cock | *el gallo* |
| spinach | *la espinaca* |
| radish | *el rábano* |
| turnip | *el nabo* |
| garlic | *el ajo* |

| | |
|---|---|
| garlic bread | *el pan de ajo* |
| parsley | *el perejil* |
| sauce | *la salsa* |
| coriander | *el cilantro* |
| mint | *la menta* |
| cucumber | *el pepino* |
| duck | *el pato* |
| French stick (bread) | *la baguette* |
| waffle | *el gofre* |
| hamburger | *la hamburguesa* |
| pasta | *la pasta* |
| egg | *el huevo* |
| salami | *el salami* |
| celery | *el apio* |
| corn | *el maíz* |
| broccoli | *el brócoli* |

## FRUITS
### *Las frutas*

| | |
|---|---|
| banana | *el plátano* |
| strawberry | *la fresa* |
| melon | *el melón* |
| orange | *la naranja* |
| peach | *el melocotón* |
| pear | *la pera* |
| apple | *la manzana* |
| grapes | *las uvas* |
| walnut | *la nuez* |
| cashew nut | *el anacardo* |

| | |
|---|---|
| date | el dátil |
| pistachio | el pistacho |
| almond | la almendra |
| lemon | el limón |
| coconut | el coco |
| apricot | el albaricoque |
| cherry | la cereza |
| mango | el mango |
| sugarcane | la caña de azúcar |
| pineapple | la piña |
| lychee | el lichi |
| pomegranate | la granada |
| guava | la guayaba |
| papaya | la papaya |
| plum | la ciruela |
| watermelon | la sandia |

## BEVERAGES
### Bebidas

| | |
|---|---|
| hot drinks | bebidas calientes |
| soft drinks | refrescos |
| coffee | el café |
| white coffee | el café con leche |
| hot chocolate | el chocolate caliente |
| tea | el té |
| lemon tea | el té con limón |
| water | el agua |
| mineral water | el agua mineral |
| fruit juice | el jugo de frutas |

| milk | la leche |
| lemonade | la limonada |
| wine | el vino |
| champagne | el champán |
| orange juice | el zumo de naranja |
| syrup | el sirope |
| green tea | el té verde |
| jasmine tea | el té al jazmín |
| soda (water) | el agua de seltz |
| whisky | el whisky |
| tomato juice | el zumo de tomate |
| pineapple juice | el zumo de piña |
| apple brandy | el licor de manzana |
| brandy | el brandy |
| cognac | el coñac |
| gin | la ginebra |
| vodka | el vodka |
| cocktail | el cóctel |
| martini | el martini |
| sherry | el jerez |
| beer | la cerveza |
| rum | el ron |

# SPICES
*Las especias*

| salt | la sal |
| pepper | la pimienta |
| red pepper | la pimienta roja |
| white pepper | la pimienta blanco |

| | |
|---|---|
| black pepper | *la pimienta negra* |
| turmeric | *la cúrcuma* |
| ginger | *el jengibre* |
| garlic | *el ajo* |
| cinnamon | *la canela* |
| cardamom | *el cardamomo* |
| cumin | *el comino* |
| cloves | *el clavo* |
| saffron | *el azafrán* |
| nutmeg | *la nuez moscada* |
| aniseed | *el anís* |
| green pepper | *la pimienta verde* |

# 34
# AT THE RESTAURANT
## EN EL RESTAURANTE

## VOCABULARY

| | |
|---|---|
| cutlery | *los cubiertos* |
| spoon | *la cuchara* |
| fork | *el tenedor* |
| knife | *el cuchillo* |
| napkin | *la servilleta* |
| table cloth | *el mantel* |
| to order | *pedir* |
| tip | *la propina* |
| menu | *el menú* |
| bill | *la cuenta* |
| waiter | *el camarero* |
| to lay the table | *poner la mesa* |
| plate | *el plato* |
| bowl | *el bol* |
| dish | *el plato* |
| casserole | *la cazuela* |
| bottle | *la botella* |
| glass | *el vaso* |
| cup | *la taza* |

| toothpick | *el palillo* |
| fresh food | *la comida fresca* |
| canned foods | *las conservas* |
| to be hungry | *tener hambre* |
| to be thirsty | *tener sed* |
| reservation | *la reserva* |
| to serve | *servir* |
| Spanish cuisine | *la cocina española* |
| Indian cuisine | *la cocina india* |
| expensive | *car@* |
| delicious | *delicios@* |
| sumptuous | *suntuos@* |
| helping | *la ración* |
| taste | *el sabor* |
| teaspoon | *la cucharilla* |

## DIALOGUE

**A** : Javier, let's eat in a restaurant today!

*¡Javier, vamos a comer en un restaurante hoy!*

**B** : In which restaurant? You want to eat in a "Tapas" restaurant or Indian food?

*¿A cuál? ¿Te apetece comer en un bar de tapas o en un indio?*

**A:** I prefer the tapas.

*Prefiero ir de tapas.*

**C** : Welcome Sir.

*Bienvenidos, señores.*

**B** : A table for two please.

*Una mesa para dos, por favor.*

**C** : Have you reserved a table?
*¿Han reservado ustedes mesa?*

**B** : Yes.
*Sí.*

**C** : Under which name?
*¿A qué nombre?*

**B** : Mr. Silberg.
*El señor Silberg.*

**A** : The restaurant is full today.
*El restaurante está lleno hoy.*

**B** : Yes there are many people.
*Sí, hay mucha gente.*

**C** : What would you like to eat for starters?
*¿Qué desean ustedes para empezar?*

**B** : Some cheese please.
*Queso, por favor.*

**C** : Would you want something to drink?
*¿Quieren ustedes algo para beber?*

**B** : One juice and one coffee.
*Un zumo y un café.*

**C** : Can I take the order?
*¿Qué van a tomar?*

**B** : After a few minutes.
*Espere un momento, por favor.*

**C** : What do you want to eat, sir?
*¿Qué quieren ustedes para comer, señores?*

**B** : Snails, a bowl of rice and chicken.
*Caracoles, un bol de arroz y pollo.*

**C** : Anything else?
*¿Algo más?*

**B** : Salad and yoghurt.
*Ensalada y yogur.*

**C** : Is that all?
*¿Eso es todo?*

**B** : Yes, for the moment.
*Sí, por el momento sí.*

**C** : What would you like for dessert?
*¿Quieren ustedes algo de postre?*

**B** : I want some chocolate cake. And you?
*Yo quiero pastel de chocolate. ¿Y tú?*

**A** : I prefer some fresh fruits.
*Prefiero fruta fresca.*

**C** : Have a good meal.
*Buen provecho.*

**B** : Please hurry.
*Dese prisa, por favor.*

**C** : Is that all for the day?
*¿Eso es todo por hoy?*

**B** : Yes, the meal was delicious.
*Sí, la comida estaba deliciosa.*

**A** : Bill please.
*La cuenta, por favor.*

C : Here you are, sir.
*Aquí está, señor.*
A : Give him a good tip.
*Dale una buena propina.*
C : Thank you very much.
*Muchas gracias.*
B : Goodbye!
*¡Adiós!*
C : See you soon!
*¡Hasta pronto!*

# 35
# AT THE POST OFFICE
## EN CORREOS

### VOCABULARY

| | |
|---|---|
| postage stamp | *el sello* |
| post card | *la tarjeta postal* |
| letter | *la carta* |
| parcel | *el paquete* |
| envelope | *el sobre* |
| money order | *el giro postal* |
| telegram | *el telegrama* |
| postal code | *el código postal* |
| address | *la dirección* |
| mailbox | *el buzón* |
| postage | *el franqueo* |
| mailbag | *la saca de correos* |
| by mail | *por correo* |
| postman | *el cartero* |
| airmail | *el correo aéreo* |
| by airmail | *por avión* |

### DIALOGUE

**A** : Where is the post office?
*¿Dónde está Correos?*

**B** : The post office is on the left.
*Está a la izquierda.*

**A** : At what time does the post office open?
*¿A qué hora abre Correos?*

**B** : The post office opens at 10 a.m.
*Abre a las diez.*

**A** : At what time does the post office close?
*¿A qué hora cierra Correos?*

**B** : The post office closes at 5 p.m.
*A las cinco.*

**A** : I want to send a parcel.
*Quiero enviar un paquete.*

**B** : By mail or by airmail?
*¿Por correo o por envío aéreo?*

**A** : I want to send this letter by post and this parcel by airmail.
*Quiero enviar esta carta por correo y este paquete por vía aérea.*

**B** : How much does it cost to mail a letter in Colombia?
*¿Cuánto cuesta enviar una carta en Colombia?*

**A:** It costs 10 euros.
*Cuesta diez euros.*

**A** : What is the postage for a letter to India?
*¿Cuál es la tarifa para enviar una carta a la India?*

**B** : It is 15 euros.
*Cuesta quince euros.*

**A** : In how many days will it reach?
*¿Cuánto tiempo tardará en llegar?*

**B** : It will reach in seven days.
*Llegará en siete días.*

**A** : Where must I put the letter?
*¿Dónde debo echar la carta?*

**B** : Put it in the mail box.
*Échela en el buzón.*

**A** : Please give me some postage stamps.
*Necesito sellos, por favor.*

**B** : Here it is. 50 euros please.
*Aquí los tiene. Son cincuenta euros.*

**A** : Where is the head office?
*¿Dónde está la oficina de correos principal?*

**B** : It is behind the post office.
*Está detrás de Correos.*

**A** : I need two postcards please.
*Necesito dos postales, por favor.*

**B** : Please check the mailing address.
*Por favor, compruebe la dirección.*

**A** : What is the postal code for India?
*¿Cuál es el código postal de la India?*

**B** : It is 11.
*El once.*

**A** : I wish to send a money-order to India.
*Quiero enviar un giro postal a India.*

**B** : For how many euros?
*¿De cuánto dinero?*

**A:** Only 500 euros.
*Sólo quinientos euros.*

# 36
# SHOPPING
## DE COMPRAS

### VOCABULARY

| | |
|---|---|
| a kilogram | *un kilo* |
| a gram | *un gramo* |
| a milligram | *un miligramo* |
| a litre | *un litro* |
| a kilometer | *un kilómetro* |
| a meter | *un metro* |
| a centimeter | *un centímetro* |
| a decimeter | *un decímetro* |
| a pound | *una libra* |
| half a kilo | *medio kilo* |

**A :** I want to go for shopping. Where is the market?
*Me gustaría ir de compras. ¿Dónde está el mercado?*

**B :** What do you want to buy?
*¿Qué quiere usted comprar?*

**A :** I want to buy clothes and fruits.
*Quiero comprar ropa y fruta.*

**B :** To buy clothes you can go to the market El Rastro and to buy fruits, go to the fruit market.
*Para comprar ropa, vaya usted al mercado El Rastro, y para la fruta, vaya al mercadillo de fruta.*

**A :** Thank you very much.
*Muchas gracias.*

**C :** Good morning ma'am, What do you want?
*Buenos días, señora. ¿Qué desea?*

**A :** Good morning. I want to buy a shirt.
*Buenos días. Quiero comprar una camisa.*

**C :** Of which colour?
*¿De qué color?*

**A :** I prefer blue.
*Busco algo azul.*

**C :** Light blue or dark blue?
*¿Azul claro u oscuro?*

**A :** Show me both.
*Enséñeme las dos.*

**C :** Here you are. But of what size?
*Aquí están. ¿Cuál es la talla?*

**A :** A large.
*Una L/grande.*

**C :** A cotton shirt or a silk shirt?
*¿Quiere usted una camisa de seda o de algodón?*

**A :** A cotton shirt. My husband doesn't like wearing silk shirts.
*De algodón. A mi marido no le gusta llevar camisas de seda.*

**C :** Anything else ma'am?
*¿Quiere usted algo más, señora?*

A : Yes, I also want a skirt and a tie.

Sí, también quiero comprar una falda y una corbata.

C : The ties are on the first floor and the skirts on the second.

Las corbatas están en la primera planta, y las faldas, en la segunda.

A : I want to buy this tie.

Quiero comprar esta corbata.

C : Sure ma'am.

Muy bien, señora.

A : How much is it for?

¿Cuánto cuesta?

C : It costs twenty euros.

Cuesta veinte euros.

A : But this is very expensive, I will see another one.

Uf, es demasiado cara. Me gustaría ver otra.

C : Do you like this tie?

¿Le gusta más esta?

A : Yes, this one is better, how much is it for?

Sí, prefiero esta. ¿Cuánto cuesta?

C : Only twelve euros.

Sólo doce euros.

A : OK. I will buy it. Where are the skirts?

Vale, la compro. ¿Dónde están las faldas?

C : Second floor.

En la segunda planta.

A : Can you please show me some silk skirts?
*¿Puede usted enseñarme faldas de seda?*

C : Which colour do you prefer?
*¿De qué color las quiere?*

A : A red skirt.
*Una falda roja.*

C : Sorry, it's not available at the moment.
*Lo siento, no tenemos ninguna en este momento.*

A : Where should I pay for the shirt and the tie?
*¿Dónde puedo pagar la falda y la corbata?*

C : At the cash counter.
*En caja.*

A : How much does that make?
*¿Cuánto es?*

C : 30 euros. / Treinta euros.

A : Here you are / Tome.

A : How much do the apples cost?
*¿Cuánto valen las manzanas?*

C : The apples cost ten euros a kg.
*Cuestan diez euros el kilo.*

A : You are asking for a lot.
*Es muy caro.*

C : The prices are fixed, ma'am.
*Los precios son los que son, señora.*

A : Give me half a kilo of apples.
*Póngame medio kilo de manzanas.*

C : Anything else?
*¿Algo más?*

A : How much are the grapes for?
*¿A cuánto están las uvas?*

C : Ten euros a kg.
*A diez euros el kilo.*

A : Are they fresh?
*¿Son frescas?*

C : Yes ma'am.
*Sí, señora.*

A : OK, then give me 2 kgs of grapes.
*Vale, póngame dos kilos de uvas.*

C : Is that all?
*¿Eso es todo?*

A : Yes, that makes it how much?
*Sí. ¿Cuánto es?*

C : 25 euros. Will you pay in cash?
*Veinticinco euros. ¿Quiere pagar al contado?*

A : Do you accept credit cards?
*¿Aceptan tarjeta de crédito?*

C : Yes ma'am.
*Claro, señora.*

A : Ah, that's good.
*¡Qué bien!*

# 37
# AT THE AIRPORT
## *EN EL AEROPUERTO*

### VOCABULARY

| | |
|---|---|
| a plane ticket | *un billete de avión* |
| economy class | *clase turista* |
| first class | *primera clase* |
| reservation | *una reserva* |
| destination | *el destino* |
| to book the luggage | *el registro de equipajes* |
| to pass at the customs | *pasar por la aduana* |
| a custom officer | *el aduanero* |
| to declare | *declarar* |
| to pay custom duty | *pagar las tasas aduaneras* |
| identification papers | *documentos de identidad* |
| a passport | *un pasaporte* |
| a visa | *un visado* |
| an identity card | *un carné de identidad / el DNI* |
| to fill a form | *rellenar un formulario* |
| a form | *un formulario* |
| luggage | *el equipaje* |
| passport control | *el control de pasaportes* |

the terminal      *la terminal*

a passenger      *un pasajero*

an immigration officer      *un agente de inmigración*

## DIALOGUE

A : How long will you stay here?

     *¿Cuánto tiempo va a quedarse aquí?*

B : I am going to be here for one month.

     *Yo voy a quedarme aquí por un mes.*

A : What is the purpose of your visit?

     *¿Cuál es la razón de su visita?*

B : I am here for holidays.

     *Estoy aquí de vacaciones.*

A : Your passport please.

     *Su pasaporte, por favor.*

B : Here is my passport.

     *Aquí está mi pasaporte.*

A : Do you have anything to declare?

     *¿Tiene alguna cosa para declarar?*

B : Yes, a small bottle of perfume and half a litre of Cuban rum.

     *Sí, un frasco pequeño de colonia y medio litro de ron cubano.*

A : Do you have any luggage?

     *¿Tiene usted equipaje?*

B : Yes, a big bag.

     *Sí, un gran bolso.*

**A :** Please show your papers.

*Los papeles, por favor.*

**B :** Here they are.

*Aquí están.*

**A :** And your visa also.

*También el visado..*

You will have to pay the custom duty.

*Tiene usted que pagar las tasas de aduana.*

Please fill the form.

*Rellene el formulario, por favor.*

**B :** I have a camera for personal use. Will I have to pay a duty on this?

*Tengo una cámara de fotos para uso personal. ¿Debo pagar los derechos de aduana por ella?*

**A :** No, no, you don't have to do that. That's fine.

*No! No! lo tiene que hacer eso. Está bien así.*

**B :** Thank you very much for your help.

*Muchas gracias para su ayuda.*

**A :** Mention not/ Welcome.

*No hay de que.*

# 38
# AT THE STATION
## EN LA ESTACIÓN

## VOCABULARY

| | |
|---|---|
| ticket | *el billete* |
| ticket machine | *la máquina de billetes* |
| information office | *la oficina de información* |
| to stamp your ticket | *validar el billete* |
| left luggage office | *la consigna* |
| corridor | *el pasillo* |
| time table | *el horario* |
| smoking compartment | *el compartimento de fumadores* |
| non-smoking | *no fumadores* |
| ticket office | *la taquilla* |
| kiosk | *el quiosco* |
| platform | *el andén* |
| reserved seat | *la reservado* |
| waiting room | *la sala de espera* |
| platform/track | *la vía* |
| wagon | *el vagón* |
| dining car | *el coche comedor* |
| first class | *Primera clase* |
| second class | *Segunda clase* |

| window seat | *el asiento de ventana* |
|---|---|
| isle | *isla* |
| one-way ticket | *de ida* |
| round trip ticket | *billet de ida y vuelta* |
| departure | *la salida* |
| arrival | *la llegada* |
| entry | *la entrada* |
| exit | *la salida* |

## DIALOGUE

**A** : The train for Santander leaves at what time?
*¿A qué hora sale el tren para Santander?*

**B** : At 10:15.
*A las diez y cuarto.*

**A** : And it arrives at what time?
*¿Y a qué hora llega?*

**B** : At 2:30.
*A las dos y media.*

**A** : Is it a direct train?
*¿Es un tren directo?*

**B** : No, you must change at Valladolid.
*No, hay que hacer transbordo en Valladolid.*

**A** : The train leaves from which platform?
*¿De qué andén sale el tren?*

**B** : It leaves from platform 2.
*Del andén dos.*

**A** : A ticket for Santander, please.
*Un billete para Santander, por favor.*

**B** : One-way or return?
   *¿Ida o ida y vuelta?*

**A** : One-way.
   *Ida.*

**B** : First class or second class?
   *¿Primera o segunda clase?*

**A** : First class.
   : *Primera clase.*

**B** : You want 'smoking' or 'non-smoking'.
   *¿Prefiere usted fumadores o no fumadores?*

**A** : Non smoking.
   *No fumadores.*

**B** : Do you want a corner seat or isle?
   *¿Quiere usted pasillo o ventana?*

**A** : I want the window seat.
   *Prefiero ventana.*

**B** : Here, your seat number is eleven.
   *Aquí tiene, su número de asiento es el once.*

**A** : Thank you very much, sir.
   *Muchas gracias, señor.*

**B** : Here is your ticket and your reservation, 300 euros.
   *Aquí tiene su billete y la reserva. Son trescientos euros.*

**A** : Thank you. Where is the waiting room?
   *Gracias. ¿Dónde está la sala de espera?*

**B** : On the left.
   *A la izquierda.*

**( 149 )**

# 39
# AT THE DOCTOR'S
## *IR AL MÉDICO*

## VOCABULARY

| | |
|---|---|
| allergy | *la alergia* |
| antibiotic | *el antibiótico* |
| AIDS | *SIDA* |
| arthritis | *la artritis* |
| appendicitis | *la apendicitis* |
| ambulance | *la ambulancia* |
| anaesthesia | *la anestesia* |
| antibacterial | *antibacteriano* |
| abortion | *el aborto* |
| acidity | *la acidez* |
| asthma | *el asma* |
| blood test | *el análisis de sangre* |
| bandage | *la venda* |
| blood transfusion | *la transfusión de sangre* |
| blood bank | *el banco de sangre* |
| blood group | *el grupo sanguíneo* |
| backache | *el dolor de espalda* |
| burn | *la quemadura* |
| bronchitis | *la bronquitis* |

| | |
|---|---|
| brain tumour | *el tumor cerebro* |
| cancer | *el cáncer* |
| chicken pox | *la varicela* |
| chronic | *crónic@* |
| contagious | *contagios@* |
| cardiovascular | *cardiovascular* |
| coronary heart disease | *la enfermedad coronaria* |
| cramp | *el calambre* |
| diabetes | *la diabetes* |
| dandruff | *la caspa* |
| dentist | *el/la dentista* |
| ear infection | *la otitis* |
| emergency | *Urgencias* |
| E.N.T. | *el otorrino* |
| electrotherapy | *la electroterapia* |
| epidemic | *la epidemia* |
| ear drops | *las gotas para los oídos* |
| eye drops | *las gotas para los ojos* |
| fracture | *la fractura* |
| gastroenteritis | *la gastroenteritis* |
| glucose | *la glucosa* |
| gynaecologist | *el/la ginecólog@* |
| gall-stone | *el cálculo biliar* |
| heart rate | *el ritmo cardíaco* |
| heart disease | *la enfermedad del corazón* |
| heart attack | *el infarto, ataque al corazón* |
| hyper tension | *la hipertensión* |
| heart transplant | *el transplante de corazón* |
| infection | *la infección* |

| | |
|---|---|
| intravenous injection | la *inyección intravenosa* |
| intramuscular injection | la *inyección intramuscular* |
| insect bite | la *picadura de un insecto* |
| hepatitis | la *hepatitis* |
| kidney-stone | el *cálculo renal* |
| mixture | el *preparado* |
| malaria | la *malaria* |
| measles | el *sarampión* |
| miscarriage | el *aborto* |
| massage | el *masaje* |
| nurse | la *enfermera* |
| nutrition | la *nutrición* |
| ointment | el *ungüento* |
| osteoporosis | la *osteoporosis* |
| paediatrician | el/la *pediatra* |
| paediatrics | la *pediatría* |
| pneumonia | la *neumonía* |
| physiotherapy | la *fisioterapia* |
| painkiller | el *calmante* |
| polio | la *polio* |
| powder | el *polvo* |
| rheumatology | la *reumatología* |
| rheumatism | el *reumatismo* |
| sleeping pill | el *somnífero* |
| smallpox | la *viruela* |
| sterilization | la *esterilización* |
| surgery | la *cirugía* |
| surgeon | el *cirujan@* |
| swelling | la *hinchazón* |

| | |
|---|---|
| sunstroke | *la insolación* |
| skin disease | *la enfermedad de la piel* |
| thermometer | *el termómetro* |
| tuberculosis | *la tuberculosis* |
| tablet | *la pastilla* |
| tetanus | *el tétanos* |
| ulcer | *la úlcera* |
| ultrasound | *el ultrasonido* |
| virus | *el virus* |
| venereal disease | *la enfermedad venérea* |
| vitamin | *la vitamina* |
| wheelchair | *la silla de ruedas* |
| X-ray | *la radiografía, el rayo-X* |
| migraine | *la migraña* |
| to be in good health | *tener buena salud* |
| to be ill | *estar enfermo* |
| to have a headache | *tener dolor de cabeza* |
| to have a toothache | *tener dolor de muelas* |
| fever | *fiebre* |
| stomach ache | *dolor de estómago* |
| throat pain | *dolor de garganta* |
| pain in the eyes | *dolor de ojos* |
| pain in the ears | *dolor de oídos* |
| to have a backache | *dolor de espalda* |
| to have a cold | *estar constipado* |
| to cure | *curarse* |
| to recover | *recuperarse* |
| soap | *el jabón* |
| cotton | *el algodón* |

| | |
|---|---|
| shampoo | *el champú* |
| aspirin | *la aspirina* |
| toothpaste | *la pasta de dientes* |
| toothbrush | *el cepillo de dientes* |
| medicine | *el medicamento* |
| injection | *la inyección* |
| lozenge | *la pastilla* |
| bandage | *la venda* |
| prescription | *la receta* |
| appointment | *la cita* |
| patient | *el paciente* |

## DIALOGUE

Doctor : How are you?
*Médico : ¿Qué le ocurre?*

Patient : I have a headache.
*Paciente : Me duele la cabeza.*

Doctor : Do you sleep well at night?
*Médico : ¿Usted duerme bien por la noche?*

Patient : No, I don't sleep well.
*Paciente : No duermo bien.*

Doctor : Ok, I'll give you medicines for your sleep and headache.
*Médico : Bueno, le voy a recetar un medicamento para el insomnio y para el dolor de cabeza.*

Patient : Doctor, I also have pain in the eyes.
*Paciente : Doctor, además me duelen los ojos.*

Doctor : Lie down, I'll put eye drops.
*Médico : Túmbese, le voy a poner unas gotas.*

Patient : Thank you doctor. How much?
*Paciente : Muchas gracias, doctor. ¿Cuánto es?*

Doctor : 100 euros and here is the prescription.
*Médico : Cien euros. Aquí tiene la receta.*

# 40
# AT THE BANK
## *EN EL BANCO*

### VOCABULARY

| | |
|---|---|
| bank account | *la cuenta bancaria* |
| bank balance | *el saldo* |
| bank book | *la libreta* |
| bank note | *el billete de banco* |
| exchange bureau | *la oficina de cambio* |
| credit card | *la tarjeta de crédito* |
| exchange rate | *el tipo de cambio* |
| a currency | *la divisa* |
| coin | *la moneda* |
| change | *el cambio* |
| traveller's cheque | *el cheque de viajero* |
| money | *el dinero* |
| cash counter | *la caja* |
| bank manager | *director(a) de banco* |
| cashier | *el cajer@* |
| account number | *el número de cuenta* |
| cheque book | *el talonario de cheques* |
| bond | *el bono* |
| loan | *el crédito* |

| U.S. Dollar | *el dólar americano* |
| Euro Dollar | *el euro dólar* |
| Canadian Dollar | *el dólar canadiense* |
| Indian Rupee | *la rupia* |
| Pound | *la libra esterlina* |
| Rouble | *el rublo* |
| Japanese Yen | *el yen* |
| bank deposits | *los depósitos bancarios* |
| bank transfer | *la transferencia bancaria* |
| bank charges | *comisión* |

## DIALOGUE

**A** : Where must I go to change the money?

*¿Dónde tengo que ir para cambiar la moneda?*

**B** : Go down there, miss – at the 'Exchange counter'.

*Vaya allí, señora, a la oficina de cambio.*

**A** : Good morning sir, I want to change a traveller's cheque, please.

*Buenos días, señor. Querría cambiar unos cheques de viajes, por favor.*

**C** : Yes, ma'am. Do you have your passport?

*Sí, señora. ¿Tiene usted a mano el pasaporte?*

**A** : Yes, here it is.

*Sí, aquí lo tiene.*

**C** : What is your address in Spain?

*¿Cuál es su dirección en España?*

**A** : C/o Mr. Rego, Iglesia Street, Orense.

*Señor Rego, calle Iglesia, Orense.*

**C** : Thank you, please sign here.
*Gracias. Firme aquí, por favor.*

**A** : I want to change some money please.
*Quiero cambiar dinero, por favor.*

**C** : Yes ma'am, which currency?
*Sí, señora. ¿Con qué divisa desea usted operar?*

**A** : The Indian Rupee.
*La rupia.*

**C** : How many do you want to change?
*¿Cuánto dinero quiere usted cambiar?*

**A** : 1000 rupees.
*Mil rupias*

**C** : Thank you; wait at the cash counter please.
*Gracias. Espere en caja, por favor.*

**A** : I want to deposit 1000 rupees in the current account.
*Quiero ingresar mil rupias en mi cuenta corriente.*

**C** : Please fill in your name and amount in the deposit slip.
*Escriba su nombre y la cantidad en la hoja de depósitos, por favor.*

**A** : What is the interest rate?
*¿Cuál es la tasa de interés?*

**C** : The interest rate is 5%.
*Es del cinco por ciento.*

**A** : Can I withdraw the fixed deposit in advance?
*¿Puedo retirar el depósito por adelantado?*

**C** : Yes, you can.

*Sí.*

**A** : Can I get a loan?

*¿Pueden darme un crédito?*

**C** : You need to fill this form.

*Tiene que rellenar este formulario.*

**A** : Can I meet the bank manager?

*Me gustaría hablar con el director de la agencia.*

**C** : Sure ma'am, you must wait for a few minutes.

*Muy bien, señora, espere unos minutos.*

# 41
# SCHOOL
## *LA ESCUELA*

## VOCABULARY

| | |
|---|---|
| to teach | *enseñar* |
| teaching | *la enseñanza* |
| to understand | *comprender* |
| to learn | *aprender* |
| a school boy | *un escolar* |
| a school girl | *una escolar* |
| nursery | *la guardería* |
| primary school | *el colegio* |
| secondary school | *la secundaria* |
| high school | *el instituto* |
| university | *la universidad* |
| library | *la biblioteca* |
| playground | *el patio* |
| canteen | *la cantina* |
| a boarding pupil | *el interno* |
| boarding school | *el internado* |
| classroom | *el aula* |
| school uniform | *el uniforme escolar* |
| laboratory | *el laboratorio* |

| | |
|---|---|
| chalk | *el gis* |
| crayon | *el crayón* |
| pencil eraser | *la goma de borrar* |
| folder | *la carpeta* |
| pen | *la pluma* |
| pencil | *el lápiz* |
| pencil sharpener | *el sacapuntas* |
| ruler | *la regla* |
| stapler | *la grapadora* |
| tape | *la cinta adhesiva* |
| thumbtack | *la chincheta* |
| glue | *el pegamento* |
| book | *el libro* |
| notebook | *el cuaderno* |
| lesson | *la lección* |
| chapter | *el capítulo* |
| timetable | *el horario* |
| lunch break | *la pausa para comer* |
| break | *el recreo* |
| vacations | *las vacaciones* |
| subject | *la asignatura* |
| modern languages | *las lenguas modernas* |
| German | *alemán* |
| English | *inglés* |
| French | *francés* |
| Spanish | *español* |
| art | *arte* |
| music | *música* |

| physical education | educación física |
|---|---|
| religious education | enseñanza religiosa |
| technology | la tecnología |
| geography | geografía |
| history | historia |
| civics | educación cívica |
| mathematics | matemáticas |
| economics | economía |
| natural sciences | ciencias naturales |
| physics | física |
| biology | biología |
| chemistry | química |
| literature | literatura |

## DIALOGUE

**A** : How many students are there in your secondary school?

*¿Cuántos estudiantes hay en tu instituto?*

**B** : There are about 700 students in our high school. It is a co-ed school.

*Unos setecientos alumnos. Es un instituto mixto.*

**A** : At what time does the class start?

*¿A qué hora empiezan las clases?*

**B** : The class starts at 8 o'clock.

*A las ocho en punto.*

**A** : What do you do in Physical Education?

*¿Qué hacéis en educación física?*

**B** : For Physical Education we go to the gym and to the sports ground.
*En educación física, vamos al gimnasio o a la pista polideportiva.*

**A** : Do you have a uniform?
*¿Lleváis uniforme?*

**B** : Yes, we wear a school uniform.
*Sí, llevamos el uniforme de la escuela.*

**A.** : At what time is the lunch break?
*¿A qué hora es la pausa para comer?*

**B** : It is at 11 o'clock and lasts for 15 minutes.
*A las once; dura un cuarto de hora.*

**A** : What is your favourite subject?
*¿Cuál es tu asignatura favorita?*

**B** : I like maths and chemistry.
*Me gustan las matemáticas y la química.*

**A** : How many holidays are there in Puerto Rico?
*¿Cuánto tiempo de vacaciones hay en Puerto Rico?*

**B** : In Puerto Rico there are about four months of vacations, in addition there are some holidays.
*En Puerto Rico hay unos cuatro meses de vacaciones, además de los días de fiesta.*

# 42
# PROFESSIONS
## *LOS PROFESIONES*

## VOCABULARY

| | Masculine | Feminine |
|---|---|---|
| doctor | *médico* | *médica* |
| professor | *profesor, catedrático* | *profesora, catedrática* |
| teacher | *maestro* | *maestra* |
| dancer | *bailarín* | *bailarina* |
| director | *director* | *directora* |
| principal | *director* | *directora* |
| singer | *cantante* | *cantante* |
| actor | *actor* | *actriz* |
| cook | *cocinero* | *cocinera* |
| tailor | *sastre* | *sastre* |
| architect | *arquitecto* | *arquitecta* |
| engineer | *ingeniero* | *ingeniera* |
| baker | *panadero* | *panadera* |
| writer | *escritor* | *escritora* |
| postman | *cartero* | *cartera* |
| policeman | *agente de policía* | *agente de policía* |
| painter | *pintor* | *pintora* |

| driver | conductor | conductora |
|---|---|---|
| politician | *político* | *política* |
| manager | *gerente* | *gerente* |
| lawyer | *abogado* | *abogada* |
| journalist | *periodista* | *periodista* |
| judge | *juez* | *jueza* |
| banker | *banquero* | *banquera* |
| clerk | *empleado* | *empleada* |
| salesperson | *vendedor* | *vendedora* |
| presenter | *presentador* | *presentadora* |
| artist | *artista* | *artista* |
| contractor | *contratista* | *contratista* |
| photographer | *fotógrafo* | *fotógrafa* |
| author | *autor* | *autora* |
| publisher | *editor* | *editora* |
| accountant | *contable* | *contable* |
| producer | *realizador* | *realizadora* |
| farmer | *agricultor* | *agricultora* |
| magician | *mago* | *maga* |
| jeweller | *joyero* | *joyera* |
| chemist | *químico* | *química* |
| blacksmith | *herrero* | *herrera* |
| goldsmith | *orfebre* | *orfebre* |
| hairdresser | *peluquero* | *peluquera* |
| gardener | *jardinero* | *jardinera* |
| fisherman | *pescador* | *pescadora* |
| carpenter | *carpintero* | *carpintera* |

| watchman | vigilante | vigilante |
| nurse | enfermero | enfermera |
| mason | albañil | albañil |
| plumber | fontanero | fontanera |
| navigator | navegante | navegante |
| cartoonist | dibujante | dibujante |
| commentator | comentarista | comentarista |
| electrician | electricista | electricista |
| computer engineer | informático | informática |
| player | jugador | jugadora |
| painist | pianista | pianista |
| researcher | investigador | investigadora |
| detective | detective | detective |
| sportsperson | deportista | deportista |
| surgeon | cirujano | cirujana |
| dentist | dentista | dentista |
| business person | empresario | empresaria |
| student | estudiante | estudiante |
| unemployed | parado | parada |

## DIALOGUE

**A** : What is your profession?
*¿En qué trabaja usted?*

**B** : I am a doctor.
*Soy médico.*

**A** : What does your father do?
*¿En qué trabaja su padre?*

**B** : My father is a dentist.
*Mi padre es dentista.*

**A** : What does your mother do?
*¿En qué trabaja su madre?*

**B** : My mother is a housewife.
*Mi madre es ama de casa.*

In Spanish, an article is never used before a profession.
*Example*:

I am *an* author.
*Soy autor.*

# 43
# CLOTHES
## *LAS ROPAS*

## MATERIAL
### *Material*

| | |
|---|---|
| cloth | *la tela* |
| wool | *la lana* |
| silk | *la seda* |
| cotton | *el algodón* |
| leather | *el cuero* |
| polyester | *el poliéster* |
| nylon | *el nylon* |

To ask about the material, we use the expression:

"¿De qué está hech@ . . . . . ."

*Example:*   What is the shirt made of?
*¿De qué está hecha la camisa?*

To mention the material, we can use two prepositions "*de*" and "*en*".

*Example:*   The shirt is made of cotton.
*La camisa está hecha **en** algodón.*
*La camisa es **de** algodón.*

( 168 )

The above two sentences can be literally translated
as :

The shirt is in cotton.
The shirt is of cotton.

## VOCABULARY

| | |
|---|---|
| costume | *el traje* |
| dress | *el vestido* |
| skirt | *la falda* |
| blouse | *la blusa* |
| scarf | *la bufanda* |
| trousers | *los pantalones* |
| shirt | *la camisa* |
| hat | *el sombrero* |
| tie | *la corbata* |
| stockings | *las medias* |
| belt | *el cinturón* |
| socks | *los calcetines* |
| coat | *el abrigo* |
| waistcoat | *el chaleco* |
| raincoat | *el impermeable* |
| jacket | *la chaqueta* |
| sweater | *el jersey, el suéter* |
| suit | *el traje* |
| t-shirt | *la camiseta* |
| underwear | *la ropa interior* |
| gloves | *los guantes* |
| sleeve | *la manga* |
| towel | *la toalla* |

| | |
|---|---|
| handkerchief | *el pañuelo* |
| shorts | *las short* |
| sports wear | *la ropa deportiva* |
| muffler | *la bufanda* |
| night suit | *el traje de noche* |
| evening dress | *el traje de noche* |
| sunglasses | *los anteojos de sol* |
| swimsuit | *el traje de baño* |
| boots | *las botas* |
| jeans | *los vaqueros* |
| shoes | *los zapatos* |
| tuxedo | *el esmoquin* |

# 44
# LODGING
## *EL ALOJAMIENTO*

## VOCABULARY

| | |
|---|---|
| a country | *un país* |
| a continent | *un continente* |
| a city/town | *una ciudad* |
| a suburb | *un barrio* |
| a village | *un pueblo* |
| a building | *un edificio* |
| a house | *una casa* |
| a flat | *un piso* |
| an apartment | *un apartamento* |
| a studio flat | *un estudio* |
| a villa | *un chalé, chalet* |
| the room | *la habitación* |
| the bedroom | *el dormitorio* |
| the kitchen | *la cocina* |
| the dining room | *el comedor* |
| the drawing room | *el salón* |
| the bathroom | *el cuarto de baño* |
| the toilet | *el servicio* |
| the entrance hall | *el vestíbulo* |

| | |
|---|---|
| the corridor | *el pasillo* |
| the attic | *el desván* |
| the garage | *el garaje* |
| the basement | *el sótano* |
| the roof | *el techo* |
| the wall | *la pared* |
| the door | *la puerta* |
| the ground floor | *la planta baja* |
| the first floor | *el primer piso* |
| the window | *la ventana* |
| the staircase | *la escalera* |
| big | *grande* |
| small | *pequeño* |
| ancient | *antigu@* |
| modern | *moderno* |
| bright | *claro* |
| dark | *oscuro* |
| isolated | *aislado* |
| calm | *tranquilo* |
| noisy | *ruidoso* |
| comfortable | *confortable, cómodo* |
| practical | *práctico* |
| to sell | *vender* |
| for sale | *en venta* |
| to buy | *comprar* |
| to rent | *alquilar* |
| landlord | *el propietario* |
| tenant | *el inquilino* |

# 45
# JEWELLERY
## *JOYAS*

## VOCABULARY

| | |
|---|---|
| a ring | *un anillo* |
| an earring | *un pendiente* |
| a bracelet | *una pulsera* |
| a pendant | *un colgante* |
| a bangle | *un brazalete* |
| a necklace | *un collar* |
| a chain | *una cadena* |
| gold | *el oro* |
| silver | *la plata* |
| diamond | *el diamante* |
| emerald | *la esmeralda* |
| ruby | *el rubí* |
| sapphire | *el zafiro* |
| turquoise | *la turquesa* |
| the pearl | *la perla* |
| opal | *el ópalo* |
| coral | *el coral* |

# DIALOGUE

**A** : I just bought a necklace.
*Me he comprado un collar.*

**B** : Made of gold or silver?
*¿De oro o de plata?*

**A** : I bought a diamond necklace and a bracelet in gold.
*He comprado un collar de diamantes y una pulsera de oro.*

**B** : My husband gave me a bracelet with emeralds and ruby.
*Mi marido me ha regalado una pulsera de rubíes y esmeraldas.*

**A** : Do you have pearl earrings?
*¿Tienes pendientes de perlas?*

**B** : I don't have real pearls but cultured ones.
*Yo notengo perlas reales sino perlas de bisutería.*

**A:** You have a beautiful collection of jewellery.
*Tienes una preciosa colección de joyas.*

# 46
# HOUSEHOLD ARTICLES AND FURNITURE
## *LOS ARTÍCULOS DE USO DIARIO y LOS MUEBLES*

## THE HOUSE HOLD GOODS
### *Los Artículos de menaje*
### VOCABULARY

| | |
|---|---|
| a cupboard | *un armario* |
| alarm clock | *el despertador* |
| a mirror | *un espejo* |
| a fan | *un ventilador* |
| an air conditioner | *un climatizador* |
| a heater | *un calefactor* |
| central heating | *calefacción central* |
| a clock | *un reloj* |
| a bedside table | *una mesilla* |
| a dressing table | *un tocador* |
| a bed | *una cama* |
| a blanket | *una manta* |
| a bedsheet | *una sábana* |
| a bedspread | *un cubrecama* |
| a pillow | *una almohada* |
| a cushion | *un cojín* |

| a washbasin | *un lavabo* |
| a bathtub | *una bañera* |
| a sink (in a kitchen) | *un fregadero* |
| a shower | *una ducha* |
| a bucket | *un cubo* |
| a soap | *un jabón* |
| a shampoo | *un champú* |
| the toothpaste | *la pasta de dientes* |
| a toothbrush | *un cepillo de dientes* |
| a razor | *una cuchilla de afeitar* |
| an electric razor | *una maquinilla de afeitar* |
| a brush | *un cepillo* |
| a comb | *un peine* |
| a detergent | *el detergente* |
| a bathroom sink | *un lavabo* |
| a toilet paper | *el papel higiénico* |
| a toilet soap | *un jabon de tocador* |
| a soup bowl | *un plato sopero* |
| a dinner plate | *un plato llano* |
| a pressure cooker | *una olla a presión* |
| a frying pan | *una sartén* |
| a teapot | *una tetera* |
| a table napkin | *una servilleta* |
| serving spoon | *cuchara de servir* |
| a fork | *un tenedor* |
| a knife | *un cuchillo* |
| a spoon | *una cuchara* |
| a teaspoon | *una cucharilla* |
| tablespoon | *cuchara de servir, cuchara grande* |

| | |
|---|---|
| soup spoon | *cuchara de sopa* |
| a washing machine | *una lavadora* |
| a dishwasher | *un lavaplatos* |
| a broom stick | *un palo de escoba* |
| an iron | *una plancha* |
| a refrigerator | *un frigorífico* |
| a microwave | *un microondas* |
| an oven | *un horno* |
| a carpet | *una alfombra* |
| crockery | *la vajilla* |
| a utensil | *un utensitio* |
| a blender | *una licuadora* |
| a toaster | *una tostadora* |
| a table | *una mesa* |
| a rocking chair | *una mecedora* |
| a chair | *una silla* |
| a bench | *un banco* |
| scissors | *las tijeras* |
| nail clippers | *el cortauñas* |

# 47
# COSMETICS
## *EL MAQUILLAJE*

### VOCABULARY

| | |
|---|---|
| sun lotion | *el bronceador* |
| a lipstick | *un lápiz de labios* |
| a nail polish | *un esmalte de uñas* |
| the powder | *los polvos* |
| an eyeliner | *un lápiz de ojos* |
| a mascara | *un rímel* |
| the eyeshadow | *la sombra de ojos* |
| a blusher | *un colorete* |
| a lipgloss | *un brillo de labios* |
| a lipsalve | *una vaselina, un cacao* |
| the perfume | *el perfume* |
| the deodorant | *el desodorante* |

# 48
# TREES
## *LOS ÁRBOLES*

## VOCABULARY

| | |
|---|---|
| a seed | *una semilla* |
| a plant | *una planta* |
| a root | *una raíz* |
| a branch | *una rama* |
| a trunk | *un tronco* |
| a leaf | *una hoja* |
| a fruit | *un fruto* |
| a flower | *una flor* |
| a bamboo | *un bambú* |
| a coconut palm | *un cocotero* |
| wood | *madera* |
| a cactus | *un cactus* |
| a tamarind | *un tamarindo* |
| a pine tree | *un pino* |
| a palm tree | *una palmera* |
| an apple tree | *un manzano* |
| a walnut tree | *un nogal* |
| a cherry tree | *un cerezo* |
| a lime tree | *un tilo* |

| | |
|---|---|
| an acacia | *una acacia* |
| a banana tree | *un banano* |
| an orange tree | *un naranjo* |
| a rubber tree | *un árbol de caucho* |
| an almond tree | *un almendro* |
| a magnolia tree | *un magnolio* |
| a pear tree | *un peral* |
| a lemon tree | *un limonero* |
| a chestnut tree | *un castaño* |
| a fig tree | *una higuera* |
| an olive tree | *un olivo* |
| a holm oak | *una encina* |
| an oak tree | *un roble* |
| a cork oak | *un alcornoque* |
| a cypress | *un ciprés* |
| a willow | *un sauce* |
| a fir tree | *un abeto* |

# 49
# FLOWERS
## LAS FLORES

## VOCABULARY

| | |
|---|---|
| a petal | un pétalo |
| a pollen | un polen |
| the white lily | la azucena |
| the lotus | el loto |
| the rose | la rosa |
| the sunflower | el girasol |
| the bluebell | la campánula azul |
| the chrysanthemum | el crisantemo |
| the orchid | la orquídea |
| the dahlia | la dalia |
| the jasmine | el jazmín |
| the camellia | la camelia |
| the azalea | la azalea |
| the daffodil | el narciso |
| the magnolia | la magnolia |
| the violet | la violeta |
| the water lily | el nenúfar |
| the daisy | la margarita |
| the dandelion | el diente de león |
| the forget-me-not | el nomeolvides |
| the snowdrop | la campanilla de invierno |

# 50
# ANIMALS
## *LOS ANIMALES*

## VOCABULARY

| | |
|---|---|
| an animal | *un animal* |
| a bird | *un pájaro* |
| an insect | *un insecto* |
| an amphibian | *un anfibio* |
| a reptile | *un reptil* |
| a mammal | *un mamífero* |
| herbivorous | *herbívoro* |
| carnivorous | *carnívoro* |
| omnivorous | *omnívoro* |
| an egg | *un huevo* |
| a tail | *una cola* |
| a fur | *un pelaje* |
| a skin | *una piel* |
| gills | *las branquias* |
| a horn | *un cuerno* |
| a trunk | *una trompa* |
| a hump | *una joroba* |
| a feather | *una pluma* |
| a claw | *una garra* |

| | |
|---|---|
| a wing | *un ala* |
| a nest | *un nido* |
| a domestic animal | *un animal doméstico* |
| a wild animal | *un animal salvaje* |
| a spider's web | *una telaraña* |
| a swallow | *una golondrina* |
| a dog bite | *una mordedura de perro* |
| a snakebite | *una mordedura de serpiente* |
| a dog | *un@ perr@* |
| a mouse | *un ratón* |
| a hamster | *un hámster* |
| a rabbit | *un conejo* |
| a cat | *un gato* |
| a horse | *un caballo* |
| a parrot | *un loro* |
| a fish | *un pez* |
| a tarantula | *una tarántula* |
| a tortoise | *una tortuga* |
| a chicken | *un pollo* |
| a cock | *un gallo* |
| a lion | *un león* |
| a tiger | *un tigre* |
| an elephant | *un elefante* |
| a crocodile | *un cocodrilo* |
| a rhinoceros | *un rinoceronte* |
| a monkey | *un mono* |
| a gazelle | *una gacela* |
| a bear | *un oso* |
| a snake | *una serpiente* |

| | |
|---|---|
| a rat | *una rata* |
| a mosquito | *un mosquito* |
| a fly | *una mosca* |
| an ox | *un buey* |
| an ant | *una hormiga* |
| a cicada | *una cigarra* |
| a caterpillar | *una oruga* |
| a butterfly | *una mariposa* |
| a dragonfly | *una libélula* |
| a grasshopper | *un saltamontes* |
| a cricket | *un grillo* |
| a spider | *una araña* |
| a flea | *una pulga* |
| a louse | *un piojo* |
| a bee | *una abeja* |
| a wasp | *una avispa* |
| a sparrow | *un gorrión* |
| a lark | *una alondra* |
| a crow | *un cuervo* |
| a canary | *un canario* |
| an eagle | *un águila* |
| a magpie | *una urraca* |
| an owl | *un búho* |
| an ostrich | *un avestruz* |
| a penguin | *un pingüino* |
| a worm | *un gusano* |
| a viper | *una víbora* |
| a grass snake | *una culebra* |
| a rattlesnake | *una serpiente de cascabel* |

| | |
|---|---|
| a lizard | *un lagarto* |
| a frog | *una rana* |
| a toad | *un sapo* |
| a duck | *un pato* |
| a cobra | *una cobra* |
| an alligator | *un caimán* |
| a buffalo | *un búfalo* |
| a camel | *un camello* |
| a centipede | *un ciempiés* |
| a crane | *una grulla* |
| a cow | *una vaca* |
| a deer | *un ciervo* |
| a dolphin | *un delfín* |
| a dragon | *un dragón* |
| an earthworm | *una lombriz* |
| a fox | *un zorro* |
| a giraffe | *una jirafa* |
| a gorilla | *un gorila* |
| a hippopotamus | *un hipopótamo* |
| a jackal | *un chacal* |
| a kangaroo | *un canguro* |
| a leopard | *un leopardo* |
| a mongoose | *una mangosta* |
| a mule | *una mula* |
| a panda | *un oso panda* |
| a pig | *un@ cerd@* |
| a scorpion | *un escorpión* |
| a sea lion | *un león marino* |
| a seal | *una foca* |

| | |
|---|---|
| a shark | *un tiburón* |
| a sheep | *una oveja* |
| a snail | *un caracol* |
| a squirrel | *una ardilla* |
| a swan | *un cisne* |
| a zebra | *una cebra* |
| a cuckoo | *un cuco* |
| a dove | *una paloma* |
| a goose | *un ganso* |
| a peacock | *un pavo real* |
| a woodpecker | *un pájaro carpintero* |
| a pigeon | *un palomo* |
| an octopus | *un pulpo* |
| an oyster | *una ostra* |
| a sea horse | *un caballito de mar* |
| a seagull | *una gaviota* |
| a seal | *una foca* |
| a wolf | *un lobo* |

# 51
# MEDIA
## LOS MEDIOS DE COMUNICACIÓN

### VOCABULARY

**PRESS**
*La prensa*

| | |
|---|---|
| a newspaper | *un periódico* |
| a daily | *un diario* |
| a weekly | *semanal* |
| a bi-monthly | *bimensual* |
| a half-yearly | *semestral* |
| an yearly | *anual* |
| a magazine | *una revista* |
| an article | *un artículo* |
| a headline | *un titular* |
| a subject | *un asunto* |
| an advertisement | *un anuncio* |
| a subscription | *una suscripción* |

**RADIO**
*La radio*

| | |
|---|---|
| a programme | *un programa* |

| | |
|---|---|
| a radio station | *una emisora (de radio)* |
| a radio set | *una radio (un transistor)* |

## TELEVISION
### *La televisión*

| | |
|---|---|
| a television set | *un televisor* |
| a colour T.V. | *un televisor en color* |
| a black & white T.V. | *un televisor en blanco y negro* |
| a screen | *una pantalla* |
| a button | *un botón* |
| a remote control | *un mando a distancia, un telemando* |

# 52
# THE FAMILY
## *LA FAMILIA*

## VOCABULARY

| | |
|---|---|
| family members | *los miembros de la familia* |
| parents | *los padres* |
| father | *el padre* |
| mother | *la madre* |
| brother | *el hermano* |
| sister | *la hermana* |
| grandparents | *los abuelos* |
| grandfather | *el abuelo* |
| grandmother | *la abuela* |
| son | *el hijo* |
| daughter | *la hija* |
| grandson | *el nieto* |
| granddaughter | *la nieta* |
| grandchild | *el niet@* |
| husband | *el marido* |
| wife | *la mujer* |
| spouse | *la esposa* |
| fiancé | *el prometido* |
| father-in-law | *el suegro* |

| | |
|---|---|
| mother-in-law | *la suegra* |
| son-in-law | *el yerno* |
| daughter-in-law | *la nuera* |
| brother-in-law | *el cuñado* |
| sister-in-law | *la cuñada* |
| aunt | *la tía* |
| uncle | *el tío* |
| neighbour | *el vecino* |
| cousin brother | *el primo* |
| cousin sister | *la prima* |
| nephew | *el sobrino* |
| niece | *la sobrina* |
| elder brother | *el hermano mayor (el primogénito)* |
| younger brother | *el hermano pequeño (el benjamín)* |
| elder sister | *la hermana mayor* |
| younger sister | *la hermana pequeña* |
| child | *el niño* |

# 53
# THE AUTOMOBILE
## EL AUTOMÓVIL

## VOCABULARY

| | |
|---|---|
| the body | *la carrocería* |
| the roof | *el techo* |
| the bumper | *el parachoques* |
| the wheel | *la rueda* |
| the tyre | *el neumático* |
| the spare wheel | *la rueda de repuesto* |
| the engine | *el motor* |
| the bonnet | *el capó* |
| the door | *la puerta* |
| the window | *la ventana* |
| the windscreen | *el parabrisas* |
| the seat | *el asiento* |
| the steering wheel | *el volante* |
| the rear-view mirror | *el (espejo) retrovisor* |
| the headlight | *el faro* |
| the number plate | *la (placa de la) matrícula* |
| the brake | *el freno* |
| the gear box | *la caja de cambios* |
| the pedal | *el pedal* |

|  |  |
|---|---|
| the clutch plate | *el embrague* |
| the accelerator | *el acelerador* |
| the indicator | *el indicador* |
| the horn | *el claxon, la bocina* |
| driving | *la conducción* |
| bus driver | *conductor(a) de autobús* |
| to drive | *conducir* |
| to accelerate | *acelerar* |
| to turn left | *girar a la izquierda* |
| to turn right | *girar a la derecha* |
| to take a U-turn | *dar cambiar de sentido* |
| to cross | *cruzar* |
| to overtake | *adelantar* |
| to brake | *frenar* |
| to stop | *parar* |
| to park | *aparcar* |
| to be out of order | *estar averiado* |
| to repair | *reparar* |
| repairing | *la reparación* |
| the garage | *el taller* |
| the mechanic | *el mecánico* |
| the service station | *la estación de servicio* |
| the petrol station | *la gasolinera* |
| petrol | *la gasolina* |
| the tank | *el tanque* |
| full | *lleno* |
| empty | *vacío* |
| to inflate | *inflar* |
| oil level | *el nivel de aceite* |

| | |
|---|---|
| tyre pressure | *la presión de los neumáticos* |
| to exceed the speed limit | *el límite de velocidad,* |
| | *exceder la velocidad permitida* |
| a fine | *una multa* |
| to cross a red light | *saltarse un semáforo* |
| to avoid an accident | *evitar un accidente* |
| to damage | *dañar* |

# 54
# TRANSPORT
## LOS TRANSPORTE

## VOCABULARY

| | |
|---|---|
| modes of transport | *los medios de transporte* |
| a vehicle | *un vehículo* |
| an automobile | *un automóvil* |
| a car | *un coche* |
| a bus | *un autobús* |
| a train | *un tren* |
| a plane | *un avión* |
| a motorbike | *una moto* |
| a cycle | *una bicicleta* |
| a metro | *un metro* |
| a boat | *una barca* |
| a ship | *un barco* |
| a truck | *un camión* |
| a bulldozer | *un bulldozer* |
| a taxi | *un taxi* |
| a bicycle | *una bicicleta* |
| a horse carriage | *un carruaje* |
| a tram | *un tranvía* |
| a trolley bus | *un trolebús* |

| | |
|---|---|
| a pick-up truck | *una furgoneta, una camioneta* |
| a tricycle | *un triciclo* |
| a tractor | *un tractor* |
| a jeep | *un jeep* |
| a van | *una furgoneta* |
| a fire engine | *un coche de bomberos* |
| an ambulance | *una ambulancia* |
| a motorboat | *una lancha* |
| a tanker | *un camión cisterna* |
| a yacht | *un yate* |
| a sailboat | *un velero* |
| a lifeboat | *un bote salvavidas* |
| a glider | *un planeador* |
| a helicopter | *un helicóptero* |
| a jet | *un reactor* |
| on foot | *a pie* |

To talk about a mode of transport, we can use any of the following ways:

1. The verbs *usar* and *utilizar* (to use). For example, Pedro uses the tram for going to the market.
   *Pedro **utiliza** el tranvía para ir al mercado.*

2. The verbs *tomar* and *coger* (to take). For example, Angel takes the bus for going to school.
   *Ángel **coge** el autobús para ir al colegio.*

3. The preposition *en* (in). For example, Beatriz goes from Barcelona to Madrid in a train.
   *Beatriz va de Barcelona a Madrid **en** tren.*

Carlos moves around in a car.
*Carlos circula **en** coche.*

But there is one exception with *pie* (foot). We use the preposition *a* instead of *en*. For example,

Mr. Antonio goes to the beach on foot.
*El señor Antonio va a la playa **a** pie.*

# 55
# COMPUTERS
## *LOS ORDENADORES*

## VOCABULARY

| | |
|---|---|
| monitor | *el monitor* |
| CPU | *CPU* |
| URL | *URL* |
| scanner | *el escáner* |
| printer | *la impresora* |
| keyboard | *el teclado* |
| hardware | *el hardware* |
| software | *el software* |
| modem | *el módem* |
| CD-ROM | *el CD-ROM* |
| floppy disk | *el disquete* |
| memory | *la memoria* |
| windows | *la ventana* |
| backup memory | *la memoria auxiliar* |
| Internet | *Internet* |
| graphics | *los gráficos* |
| multimedia | *multimedia* |
| information technology | *la informática* |
| hard disk | *el disco duro* |

| | |
|---|---|
| processor | *el procesador* |
| RAM | *RAM* |
| database | *la base de datos* |
| mouse | *el ratón* |
| drive | *la unidad de disco* |
| speakers | *los parlantes* |
| DOS | *DOS* |
| microphone | *el micrófono* |
| laser printer | *la impresora láser* |
| to install | *instalar* |
| to download | *descargar* |
| mouse pad | *la alfombrilla* |
| downloading | *la descarga* |
| installation | *la instalación* |
| data | *los datos* |
| sound card | *la tarjeta de sonido* |
| hard disk drive | *la unidad de disco duro* |
| the graphic representation | *la representación gráfica* |
| graphical user interface | *el interfaz gráfico* |
| Internet café | *el cibercafé* |
| e-mail | *el correo electrónico* |
| CD-ROM drive | *la unidad de CD-ROM* |
| software engineer | *el ingeniero informático* |